Books by J · Edgar Hoover

Persons in Hiding
Masters of Deceit
A Study of Communism
Communism

Communism

J·Edgar Hoover

on

Communism

RANDOM HOUSE, New York

Acknowledgment is hereby made to the following for permission to reprint from their works:

Holt, Rinehart and Winston, Inc. for *A Study of Communism*, by J. Edgar Hoover. Copyright © 1962 by Holt, Rinehart and Winston, Inc. For *Masters of Deceit*, by J. Edgar Hoover. Copyright © 1958 by J. Edgar Hoover.

Kappa Delta Pi, An Honor Society in Education, for "Unmasking the Communist Masquerader," by J. Edgar Hoover, from *The Educational Forum*, May, 1950.

Columbia for "The Deadly Contest," by J. Edgar Hoover, August, 1961.

The Methodist Publishing House for "Time of Testing," by J. Edgar Hoover, from *Christian Action*.

Harvard Business Review for "The U.S. Businessman Faces the Soviet Spy," by J. Edgar Hoover.

Christian Herald for "Let's Fight Communism Sanely," by J. Edgar Hoover. Copyright © 1961 by J. Edgar Hoover. For "The Communist War Against Human Dignity," by J. Edgar Hoover. Copyright © 1963 by J. Edgar Hoover.

*T*his book is dedicated to my associates in the FBI whose devotion to duty has played such a vital role in the fight against communism. America owes a deep debt of gratitude to these men and women for their selfless efforts in helping to preserve our nation's heritage of freedom.

A Note to the Reader

Mr. J. Edgar Hoover, the Director of the Federal Bureau of Investigation, is the nation's foremost authority on the danger of communism within the borders of the United States. Mr. Hoover, as a young attorney in 1919 for the Department of Justice, studied the earliest documents of communism to prepare legal briefs for the Attorney General. Since 1924, as head of the FBI, Mr. Hoover has followed closely the ramifications of this conspiracy. No man in America can claim a greater knowledge of this twentieth-century conspiracy.

Mr. Hoover has prepared a short essay introducing a compilation of selected quotations from his published writings and speeches dealing with communism during the period of its existence in the United States. In this essay, the FBI Director discusses briefly the historical background of the Communist Party in this country, but concentrates chiefly on the Communist Party, U.S.A., of the 1960's. The reader will learn that this Party, led by its General Secretary, Gus Hall, has developed tactical changes, changes of style and look, to gain a respectability. At heart, however, it remains the same instrument of Soviet control and tyranny.

This compendium of Mr. Hoover's views has value for both scholars and members of the general public who are interested in the development of world communism. The quotations, given chronologically within each subject, deal with over twenty different aspects of the communist assault against our institutions. The reader is enabled, therefore, to determine the Party's views and position relative to such areas, for example, as religion, life in the Communist Party, and relations with the Soviet Union. The source for each quotation is given if the reader would like to study the particular subject more fully.

The quotations will show the basic purpose of the Party in this country—namely, that it is an agent of the Soviet Union in our midst. Here lies its original aim. Here is its present purpose.

Mr. Hoover's essay and quotations will recall for all patriotic citizens the absolute necessity of their being vigilant, alert, and willing to do their share to defeat this conspiracy. Even after fifty years, the battle is not over.

Contents

1

*Communism
Today*

An Appraisal

THE PARTY'S NEW LOOK

Not long ago a college student visited my office. He was interested in talking about communism and its threat to the American nation. During our conversation this serious young man asked: "Is communism today different from what it was fifty years ago? Has it changed? Is it still a danger to us internally?"

My mind flooded back almost a half century. I remembered the days, weeks, and months when I, as a young Special Assistant to the Attorney General, had studied a Russian-born adventurer by the name of Ludwig C.A.K. Martens, who had come to the United States and proclaimed himself the "official" representative of the new Bolshevik regime of V.I. Lenin.

Martens was an exotic, bizarre, picturesque character—but his significance lay in the fact that he was the prototype of a new kind of ideology, a new kind of mentality which was to infect our American life. Martens, a personal friend of top Bolshevik leaders, was to exemplify the effort by a foreign power, the Soviet Union, to propagandize, subvert, and attempt to overthrow our institutions of free society. No wonder the

4

Russian Bolshevik Federation in America hailed Martens' presence in the United States as "an opportunity of revolutionary activity in direct contact and cooperation with the Russian proletariat and Soviet Government of Russia."

Martens' office was at 299 Broadway in New York City. His command of English was poor. He was constantly in need of money, and in 1920 it was learned that his presence was being financed from Moscow by means of smuggling diamonds into the United States. Seaman couriers brought Martens' letters and directives from the Comintern.

As I think of Ludwig C.A.K. Martens—one of the first communists in the country—with his ill-fitting clothes, his clandestine movements in Lower Manhattan, his hit-and-miss activities, I am tempted to smile in almost disbelief. Here was communism in its early beginnings in the United States (the Communist Party, U.S.A., was founded in September, 1919). These early comrades were mostly foreign-born, had few contacts with American culture, spent most of their time arguing among themselves concerning the doctrine of Marxism-Leninism, about which they understood little in depth.

I smile in disbelief because today—a half century later—their successors dress in excellent clothes, are mostly native-born, and have received widespread attention from the American people. Gus Hall, the Minnesota-born General Secretary of today's Communist Party, U.S.A., recently stated that he had contacted through radio, television and personal appearances approximately fifty million Americans.

Martens (and other early Party leaders in this country, such as John Reed, Benjamin Gitlow, and Charles Ruthenberg) had limited contact in regard to communism with native Americans. In fact, they did not want publicity. The early Party was largely underground, its meetings secret. *The Communist* (an organ of the Party) once referred to a meeting of the comrades as taking place "Sometime recently, somewhere between the Atlantic and Pacific, between the Gulf and the Great Lakes. . . ." The Party's influence on American life was minimal, virtually nonexistent.

Yet today we see Hall widely feted on college and university campuses as he comes to make speeches. Herbert Aptheker (the Party's theory expert) is accepted in top academic circles, where he discourses on communist history and reads papers on Negro history. The Party's paper, the *Daily World,* is published five days a week, with little advertising, and achieves a wide distribution. The Party holds a special convention in New York City, with delegates from across the country, amid accompanying press, radio, and television coverage.

How has the Party been able in various ways to spread its influence so widely? Why do many people consider the Party a legitimate political party within our democratic society?

How has the Party changed from the days of Mar-

tens and John Reed to the current Gus Hall? This was
the question the college student asked me. What are
the dangers of the Party—remembering that the Party
today, the same as in the days of Martens, remains the
faithful and obedient servant of the Soviet Union.

The American people, I feel, need to know more
factually about what the Communist Party and its
minions are doing today. This is a changing world, with
powerful forces buffeting all nations and peoples. Communism in this country, as well as communism internationally, has been vitally affected by nationalism, the
break between the Soviet Union and Red China, the
rise of the so-called Third World, and the Soviet invasion of Czechoslovakia in August, 1968. In our own
nation, the last decade has seen a growing urbanization,
the rise of the civil rights movement, the war in Vietnam, the unrest on college campuses, the New Left
student movement, the breakdown of law and order, the
increase in crime, and the wide acceptance of the perni-
cious concept of civil disobedience.

In my two books, *Masters of Deceit* (1958) and *A
Study of Communism* (1962), I sketched the rise of
communism in this country, its efforts to penetrate our
institutions and to create a "communist man," an obedient robot, as the weapon of revolution. Since these
books, many changes have occurred in the communist
movement, changes which reflect *how communism is attempting tactically to adapt to changing national and
international conditions to effect its basic aim of overthrowing our free government.* As we will see, com-

munism has changed in many ways; yet it remains basically the same. In outward dress, speech, and habits Martens looked much different from the well-dressed, poised Gus Hall. But in their hearts beats the same purpose—that of communist revolution.

THE TRAUMA OF 1956— DESTALINIZATION

To understand Gus Hall and his Communist Party of today, to see how communism has changed in many ways in the last decade—yet remains the same fundamental danger to our free society—we must first briefly cast our eyes backward.

The Party's first decade in the United States was chiefly one of becoming orientated, that is, emerging from an underground existence, recruiting a native cadre, and perfecting an organizational structure. From the Party purges of 1928–1929 (when such top leaders as James P. Cannon, Jay Lovestone, and Benjamin Gitlow were expelled) until 1956 the Party more and more assumed a *Stalinist* pose. Joseph Stalin, operating through the Comintern, enforced his will on the Communist Party, U.S.A., creating an obedient Party, fully loyal to the Soviet Union.

Pursuant to Moscow, the tactics of the Party conformed to the expedient needs of the day, as exemplified by its promotion of a united front against fascism during the 1930's, its justification of the Soviet-Nazi "non-aggression" pact in 1939, its support of the American war effort during World War II, its reversion to a hard anti-American line following the Duclos article* in 1945, its endorsement of the policy of "peaceful co-existence" after Stalin's death, and its condoning of the suppression of Hungary in 1956 and Czechoslovakia in 1968.

Top Party officials, such as William Z. Foster, were completely uncritical in their acceptance of Soviet policy. In 1951, when the U.S. Supreme Court upheld convictions of Party leaders for violation of the Smith Act, the Party plunged underground. Offices were closed, strict security measures imposed, its organizational structure decentralized. Stalin died in 1953, but the Party here continued in his image as a highly disciplined, hard-core, obediently loyal organization.

The massive turning point in the history of the Communist Party, U.S.A.—and communism internationally—came in June, 1956, an event which not only was to shock, stun, and confound the membership, but was to drastically shape the Party in the years ahead.

In that month the Party membership learned in the public press of Nikita Khrushchev's famous speech denouncing Stalin. Khrushchev accused Stalin —revered and worshipped as a god by millions of communists—of being, in actuality, a liar, thief, mur-

* Jacques Duclos, Secretary of the Communist Party of France, in April, 1945, in an article in a French Communist journal, denounced the Communist Party, U.S.A.'s policy of working with capitalism as "revisionism" and hence a betrayal of Marxism-Leninism. Based on Duclos' criticism, the Party initiated a purge in its ranks and became more militant.

derer, and an enemy of communism! (Khrushchev actually made his speech in February, 1956, at the 20th Congress of the Russian Communist Party in secret session, but the text of his remarks came into the possession of the outside world and was published in June, 1956, by our Department of State.)

"Horrible!" exclaimed one Party leader. "How could this happen in a society which was building socialism?" The late Eugene Dennis, General Secretary of the Party, who had just "given" three and a half years of his life in prison for the Party for violating the Smith Act, wrote in anger:

> Nothing can justify the use of tortures and rigged trials; large-scale deportations . . . the persecution of the Jewish doctors and snuffing out the lives of more than a score of Jewish cultural figures.

The Party was drastically affected by the trauma of June, 1956.

Actually, destalinization had a paradoxical effect on the Party, triggering two major trends, seemingly contradictory.

After the Khrushchev revelations many Party leaders and members began "dropping out," "fading away"—chagrined, embarrassed, disillusioned. Some had devoted all of their lives to what they felt was a movement for the betterment of humanity, and now what did they find: anti-Semitism, persecution, brutality!

In this process, a bitter factionalism erupted. John

Gates, an old-time Party veteran, then serving as acting
National Executive Secretary and also editor-in-chief
of the *Daily Worker,* advocated an outspoken critical attitude toward the Soviet Union. "Why must we jump
on the USSR bandwagon?" Gates asked, when everyone now knew the deplorable situation there. No
longer, he argued, should everything coming from Russia be blindly accepted.

William Z. Foster, the patriarch of the Party, on
the other hand, advocated a sheepish compliance with
the new conditions. Other leaders attempted to minimize criticism of the Kremlin and tried to find "an-
swers" for the errors committed by Stalin.

In this time of trouble (June, 1956, to December,
1959) key issues striking at the heart of communism
were debated:

To what extent should the Party in this country
criticize the Soviet Union? What kind of organization
should the Party be? Should it be a tightly knit, disciplined Party (the Leninist-Stalinist type), or more
open, broad-based, and nationalist in sentiment (as
Gates wanted)? How far should self-criticism be carried?
What about anti-Semitism in the Soviet Union?

The growing ascendancy, however, of a pro-Soviet
faction inside the Party gave a final answer to the
time of trouble. Aided by the voluntary departure
(January, 1958) of Gates—who subsequently rejected
communism in favor of liberal democracy and the
values of a free and open society—and others of his

liberal views, plus Party-directed purges, the pro-Soviets won the battle decisively.

The pro-Soviet faction was headed by a powerful, dynamic, and resolute leader by the name of Gus Hall. A former head of the Ohio State Communist Party and National Secretary, Hall had been in the underground and had served a prison sentence for violation of the Smith Act. He now moved into the leadership vacuum at the Party's 17th National Convention in December, 1959. With Hall's election as General Secretary at this convention, a stability based on unswerving allegiance to the Soviets again settled over the Party. Today's Party is the image of this Moscow-trained steelworker who attended the Lenin School and who in a court trial was asked:

Q. And you are willing to fight and overthrow this government?
A. Absolutely.
Q. And you are willing to take up arms and overthrow the constituted authorities?
A. When the time comes, yes.

Ironically, destalinization created a second major trend. We see today a Party obediently loyal to the Soviets (in fact, one of the most devoted of all the communist parties of the world), yet a Party which bears the marks of tactical change dictated by the shocks of destalinization and the agonizing period of troubles, factionalism, and debate over change and re-

formism. After Khrushchev's speech the old Stalinist-
type Party was no more, and all the king's horses and
all the king's men could not put it back together again
in its original form—nor did Hall want to!

"WHAT IS TO BE DONE?"

Not long ago one of our confidential
sources told an interesting story. A Party meeting was
being held at a private home in an Eastern city. During the discussion a group of books on a nearby table
suddenly slipped and fell to the floor. Among the books
was a little pamphlet by Lenin entitled "What Is To
Be Done?" One of the participants, picking up this
pamphlet, held it aloft and said to the others: "Comrades, here is the problem. What is to be done?"

"What is to be done?" Here was Gus Hall's problem in early 1960 after he became the undisputed
leader of the Party with his election as General Secretary.

Hall—and others—realized that the Party, in order
to survive, had to achieve an updating, a new image—
quickly and in great depth. Moreover, this new image
must be designed to make the Party more relevant to
American society, to the burgeoning changes of the
1960's. In this process the Party had to be made more
palatable to the great mass of the American people,
especially to youth, labor, and the intellectual community.

This new image concept, to Hall, had a twofold

approach: *First,* the new image must wash away the telltale, brutal stains of Stalinism, with its concentration camps, anti-Semitism, and abuse of human rights, later compounded by the ugliness of Soviet intervention in Hungary (October, 1956), the crackdown by the Soviets against liberal authors, and Moscow's Cold War behavior in foreign policy. *Second,* the new image must project a Party posing as indigenous Americans, working for the best interests of the people, and urging a "non-violent" and "constitutional" arrival of "socialism" (meaning communism) in this country through the will of the people.

"History also bears witness," Hall recently told a North Dakota university audience, "that the form of this new social structure will not be a transplant. U.S. socialism will be molded by our experience as a nation, as a people. Our socialism will be molded by our experiences with the Constitution and the Bill of Rights. It will reflect our experiences with a multiple-party system. It will reflect our trade union experience.

"And when socialism comes onto the agenda, I am convinced that the majority of you in this hall tonight will not only be for it but will be advocating it—and helping to make it work."

Hence, since 1960 we have seen an almost desperate striving for legitimacy by the Party, an effort to gain acceptance by the people as a respected element of American democratic society.

For a Party which stems from individuals like Ludwig C.A.K. Martens, William Z. Foster, and Elizabeth Gurley Flynn, this is indeed a tall order—almost unbelievable.

To understand what happened in developing the post-Stalinist Party, we must realize that the Party went to the "grass roots" in a big way—that is, it deliberately and systematically went out to meet people and gain influence.

Looking out over Manhattan from his third-floor office at national Communist Party headquarters at 23 West 26th Street, Gus Hall could dream of making personal contacts with businessmen, stockbrokers, merchants, Chambers of Commerce, service clubs, trade associations—those elements of the so-called capitalist class against whom Marx and his successors had inveighed for so long.

But from these groups came no invitations, to Hall or other Party officials, to attend conventions, banquets, or meetings. To the Party, the landscape looked bleak. Where could it meet prominent and respected Americans, people who would listen to its propaganda message, and where lay the possibility of exerting an influence?

Hall's task was complicated by the fact that the Government had instituted prosecution against the Party under the Internal Security Act of 1950, which, in essence, had the purpose of making the Party, its officers, and its members register with the Attorney General. On June 5, 1961, the United States Supreme Court upheld the constitutionality of the registration provision of the Act. To publicly identify oneself as an officer or member of the Party could mean possible prosecution.

Whether it can be called Hall's luck or Hall's initiative, it is difficult to say, but the magic key which was to open up the cold and forbidding locks of the capitalist world was close at hand.

Here is what happened.

In August, 1960, the Party's National Executive Committee held a high-level conference in New York City. At this meeting Daniel Rubin, the National Youth Secretary, advocated the holding of a national youth conference. Why? To establish a new Marxist youth group. (The Labor Youth League, the Party's youth front, which had followed the Young Communist League and the American Youth for Democracy, had disappeared just after the Party's period of underground activity.)

A new youth group should be established—and soon! As a result, Rubin made an extended tour of the nation, visiting a number of college campuses.

Out of this effort the Party's program for speaking at colleges was born—a program which was to become the Party's major weapon for achieving its "new look" and respectability. Even Party leaders did not visualize what a bonanza communism was to reap in this field and how, through this initial breakthrough into the noncommunist world, other avenues of contact were to develop.

Rubin was invited to give a speech on a campus. Then Herbert Aptheker. Then Hyman Lumer, Benjamin J. Davis, Jr., Carl Winter, Elizabeth Gurley Flynn, and James Jackson, all top Party officials. In these early days Party spokesmen (because of the Internal Security Act of 1950) were careful not to identify themselves publicly as communist officials. Rubin presented himself as editor of *New Horizons for Youth,* a Party youth paper. Aptheker billed himself as editor of *Political Affairs,* the Party's theoretical journal.

At first Party speakers attempted, basically, to arouse student and faculty interest in the Party and communism. But soon, as Aptheker reported, Party leaders found their campus receptions cordial and friendly. In due course they were making speeches about current international and national events, about history, philosophy, social conditions, even religion, giving the communist viewpoint.

By the beginning of the 1962–63 academic year the Party had established a "Lecture and Information Bureau" in New York City under the direction of Arnold Samuel Johnson, the Party's Public Relations Director. (His title indicates the basic purpose of the speaking program.) Letters over Johnson's signature were sent to college and university groups throughout the country. "We have speakers available," they said in essence. "If you are interested, please let us know."

As a result, from 1961 to the present, Party leaders have made over 360 public appearances before campus groups, with audiences ranging from a few to, in one instance, over 12,000.

The speaking program gave the Party entree into the intellectual community—the very area where it was able not only to reach thousands of students, faculty members, and others, but, in the interests of academic freedom, it also had an audience willing to listen. If Rubin or Hall had set up a soapbox in Central Park in New York City, in Lafayette Square in Washington, or in Pershing Square in Los Angeles, how many people would have listened? A mere handful at most.

Master propagandists that they are, Party leaders soon saw the proper approach to make in their speeches. They posed as protectors of the Constitution (especially the rights guaranteed by the Bill of Rights). They claimed they were furthering academic freedom, and they presented communism as a democratic philosophy, denying that it was a criminal conspiracy or tied to a foreign power. If, as sometimes happened, they were not permitted to speak by school authorities, they suddenly became "martyrs," crying crocodile tears about the denial of the rights of free speech. Any controversy over their appearance was exploited by Party publicists.

Herbert Aptheker is a Ph.D., an author of many books, widely versed in Marxist theory and practice. He became the Party's "intellectual" battering ram on campuses. His academic background gave him status. "The audience was very receptive to Aptheker," a listener commented, "and it is not difficult to see why. He is certainly a most formidable spokesman for communism. He presents an impressive appearance. He was meticulously dressed in the manner of a conservative banker. He is a cool and deliberate speaker, with a firm, forceful, though usually soft, voice which is not without its effects on the audience."

Aptheker—and other Party leaders—did everything possible in their speeches to make communism intellectually respectable: to peel off the old layers of Stalinism and brutality, the criticisms of Marxism as outdated, irrelevant, perverted, and barbaric. Instead they tried to show communism as a "scientific," enlightened, creative way of life which, through peaceful means, would bring this nation to a more humane, just, and prosperous society. Capitalistic "evils" would be liquidated while new, undreamed avenues of human accomplishment would be opened up for mankind!

No wonder a listener could say of Aptheker: "Everyone in attendance seemed to be impressed by what he said . . . Students were overheard to say: 'How could I possibly live in this country without seeing these evils?' 'Everything the man says makes sense; he must be wrong, but where?' "

Let's be frank. College students and faculties were not swept off their feet by communist presentations. Many students went out of curiosity. "What does a real, live communist look like?" Perhaps there was a fad to allow off-beat-type speakers to appear. Student after student was unimpressed with both the academic and forensic abilities of the speakers—who were frequently heckled and questioned vigorously. "I couldn't believe," one Pennsylvania student said, "how stupid the arguments of communism were until I heard Gus Hall."

Yet, from the Party's viewpoint, the speaking program served as an excellent channel to gain access to a large segment of America's noncommunist population.

The story is not yet complete. Almost invariably these college appearances opened doors to other areas of personal contact.

First, there was radio and television. Hall was frequently interviewed as a "prominent public figure" by the press, radio, and television. His speech (or later interview) might be broadcast. The student and metropolitan press would carry stories—and often elicit subsequent editorials, letters to the editor, cartoons, feature articles. Even though the vast majority of the comments were hostile to the Party, many editorials defended the right of the Party leader to speak—thereby indirectly giving him a certain degree of respectability. Hall, in particular, liked to participate in late-hour radio programs during which questions from the public were received. Even though he was often violently attacked, he relished citizen concern and interest in what he had to say.

PROPELLED TO A LARGER STAGE

Even communists think in terms of gold. A top Party official surveying the speaking program commented: "These appearances have cost us a lot of time, inconvenience, and effort. But they have been pure gold."

This valuation is highly accurate. The initial breakthrough of the capitalist dike by these appearances in 1960 and 1961 propelled the Party onto a wider and more effective stage of national life and gave it an aura of increasing respectability.

In an area difficult to assess, it opened the doors for increased influence in university and scholarly circles. The Party is today operating an academic vehicle, the American Institute for Marxist Studies (AIMS), which, under Herbert Aptheker's guidance, publishes documents, contacts university personnel, and works subtly to legitimize communist theory. Aptheker has participated in a variety of academic meetings with reputable noncommunist scholars.

Mention should be made of the Party's effort to capitalize on studies of the so-called "young Marx," that is, the writings of Karl Marx as a young man (before he had developed his more advanced theories of communism). In these writings, says the Party, are found the real compassion, understanding, and tolerance of Marxism which have subsequently been corrupted by successors such as Stalin and his henchmen. Communism, it is alleged, is not barbarism, but, as originally conceived by Marx, humanism.

In still another area of importance the Party makes an effort to achieve a type of modus vivendi with religion. Why should religious leaders be afraid of com-

munism, the Party asks? The Party, it claims, works for the same basic objectives as the church: the dignity of man, the elimination of social evils, peace on earth.

Herbert Aptheker participated with churchmen and university professors in a three-day "Christian-Marxist Dialogue." Introduced as a communist theory expert, Aptheker told the group, among other things, that "A red thread runs through the history and teaching of Christianity. The church, like communism, is based on revolutionary ideas." He also said:

> "Originally the church was working in the communist tradition—for change. We both demand justice on earth."

> "This is the post-religious phase of history. Religion has been in a crisis since the 1917 revolution."

> "The West will be the grave of God. The present capitalistic ties of Christianity tie it to a corpse, not a living God."

The Party today—as in the past—is careful not to openly denounce religion as the "opium of the people" (fearing to alienate Americans), but it aggressively seeks to say that Marxism has goals identical with religion (the Judaeo-Christian tradition) and that church leaders should start a dialogue with the Party—which, of course, would give great respectability to the post-Stalinist Party. This is why *Political Affairs* devoted its entire issue of July, 1966, to articles discussing communism and religion.

In the field of public life, the Party has taken steps to gain acceptability. Here, the ground has been difficult. The Party has run candidates for public office, such as William C. Taylor, Vice-Chairman of the Party's Southern California District, a candidate for the Board of Supervisors of Los Angeles County in 1964. Though running as an independent, Taylor did not attempt to conceal his communist affiliations. He received over 33,000 votes—meaning that he was defeated, but the Party felt a public relations victory had been achieved.

Dorothy Healey, Chairman of the Party's Southern California District, ran for Tax Assessor of Los Angeles County in 1966. Herbert Aptheker was a candidate the same year for Congress from the 12th Congressional District in Brooklyn.

At a special national convention in July, 1968, the Party nominated Charlene Alexander Mitchell, a Negro, for President of the United States, and Michael Zagarell as Vice-President. Zagarell was only twenty-three years of age and hence constitutionally ineligible to hold office. However, the convention overlooked this point, since it had a more primary purpose in mind: to attract Negro support (through Mitchell) and the attention of youth (through Zagarell). The Party's aim, understandably, is not only to elect its candidates, where possible, but to fan out its propaganda, influence, and personal contacts through an election campaign.

Then there was the matter of a press outlet to the general public. Since the days of Lenin the printing press has been not only a means of enforcing discipline and control inside the Party, but also a transmission belt to the general public. Hall's post-Stalinist Party agreed with Lenin. The aim now was to make the Party's press less sectarian, less narrow and dogmatic, and more appealing to the noncommunist, the fellow who might read a copy of its newspaper.

The post-1960 Party took steps to increase the firing power of its press. The *Daily Worker*, which had been reduced to one edition a week (and became known as *The Worker*), in January, 1958, because of financial troubles, was now (September, 1961) increased to two issues a week. But this was not enough. A daily paper with a more appealing format had to reappear:

"The need for a Marxist daily press," Hall proclaimed, "is more critical now than at any time in our history—and it is needed more in the U.S.A. than in any other part of the world, for the heart of world imperialism is here. This country is capitalism's nerve center, its control room."

Not until July, 1968, did the Party's new paper, the *Daily World*, make its appearance. The financial cost is tremendous—considering there is little advertising. But the Party today, thanks to bountiful legacies in wills, is reasonably affluent. This money, its leadership feels, can best be put to use in a daily paper appealing to the noncommunist. The new paper is larger, more cleverly edited, and through increased coverage of cultural, literary, and sporting events, has a decided noncommunist appeal.

This projection onto a wider national stage has compelled the Party to maintain a public relations service at national headquarters. Here press releases are issued. Inquiries from newsmen for interviews, statements, and background material are handled. Hall often will utilize a press interview to convey some particular point he wants publicized throughout the country. In addition, the Party handles a large volume of mail from citizens making inquiries about the Party and its position on current matters.

The internal structure of the Party reflects the New Look. Great effort has been made to dispel the "underground mentality" of both the leadership and the membership. For years the Party operated largely as a clandestine organization, shunning publicity and personal contacts with the noncommunist world. To be a communist automatically meant a behavioral pattern of stealth, fear, and cunning. The Party still has an underground (and must always maintain one because of its illicit activities, such as secret contacts with the Soviet Union, the handling of financial angels, the concealment of the identities of some key Party members), but the emphasis now is for the rank-and-file membership to "assimilate" and "make personal contacts." The member is being urged to be more open, friendly, and persuasive, to sell the daily paper, to recruit.

An old-time member doesn't learn new attitudes quickly—but the Party is on its way. Security measures, so prominent during the underground period of the 1950's, are being relaxed. Since the courts have virtually declared null and void Federal anticommunist legislation, the Party does not hesitate to conduct many of its activities openly. Internal discipline is being refined to meet post-Stalinist needs. Membership cards have been abandoned. The Party structure has been decentralized. The member's loyalty is still maintained through ideological indoctrination (there has been no lessening of the emphasis on Marxist-Leninist indoctrination for members), but the Party is less dogmatic in enforcing discipline through threats and threatened expulsions, as in the pre-1956 period.

Destalinization has been a sledgehammer battering at the Party—affecting both its internal and external positions. Little perhaps did Nikita Khrushchev realize in 1956, when he took the rostrum at the Soviet Party's 20th Congress, how significant and lasting his words would be. But by besmirching the "god of communism," he set in motion waves of change and counterchange which are still lapping at the feet of the Party in this country today.

THE BIG "R" OF COMMUNISM

Vladimir Lenin liked to scribble notes. He would jot down on scraps and pieces of paper his innermost thoughts. Historians have gleaned insights of communism's future line of actions from points written down by a man whose whole life was centered on the burning question: "How do I bring about a communist revolution?"

If Gus Hall is today keeping a diary, he is jotting down his worries about the big "R" of communism—Revolution. Why the New Look Party of post-1960? Why the attempt to meet and influence people? Why the attempt to make the Party's program more relevant to today's society?

For Gus Hall, the New Look changes have only one basic purpose—to promote an ultimate communist revolution in this country. To the hard-core Marxists in America, the "new style" program is not designed to promote legitimate reforms in society. *Rather, the Party's post-Stalinist format is to create conditions which, sooner or later, will bring about a communist transformation of our capitalist-democratic society.*

Hence, to view the communist concern in social and economic problems, in racial unrest, in eliminating poverty, disease, and discrimination as an effort to effect legitimate reform is to miss the real inner purpose of the Communist Party, U.S.A. The post-Stalinist New Look Party is as dedicated to communist revolution as was the Stalinist Party. The only thing that has changed is the external or publicly displayed style of clothes.

For this reason, a recent Party secret memorandum, emphasized that there was an "urgency of advancing the struggle to new levels"—meaning that the Party's aim in participating in the issues of the day, such as the civil rights movement, the New Left student movement, opposition to the war in Vietnam, is to emphasize how these movements can be moved to bring about the "big R."

For Hall, the prism of vision of today's society is that of the Marxist concept of "class," "class struggle," and "radicalization of the masses." How can the New Left, black-power advocates, and trade-union leaders be guided toward the "big R"? "To reach this destination," the secret memorandum says, "greater clarity is required on such questions as the class nature of the 'Establishment,' the historic role of the working class, and the centrality of the Negro question and its relationship to the class struggle and the fight for peace." Another quotation:

> To make clear the class basis of the war, of the economic problems of the workers, of racism and national oppression—this is why the Communist Party is needed.

Only the Communist Party, with its "science of Marxism-Leninism," Hall feels, can lead the revolutionary struggle in this country. All other elements, though claiming the revolutionary label, are imposters, ill-equipped, or romantics.

To carry out its mission of the "big R," the Party must recruit—now.

"In the face of these needs the sheer numerical inadequacy of the Communist Party to fulfill them and the necessity to add thousands of new communists to its ranks become increasingly evident," the memorandum adds. "To build our Party is not a narrow partisan outlook; it is an urgent necessity for the future of our country."

The Party's current dilemmas, problems, and maneuverings reflect its effort to bring a Marxist viewpoint and leadership to our national life today. In our current society, with its violence, chaos, and uncertainty, the Party has its best opportunity for exploitation since the depression days of the 1930's.

THE CHAOTIC ISSUES OF THE DAY

The chaotic issues of the day—the student New Left, ghetto riots, black power, the rise of extremism, violence in society, the war in Vietnam, the increase in crime, the breakdown of law and order—have presented perplexing problems and dilemmas. "It was a lot easier to run the Party back in the days of William Z. Foster," said one comrade recently. The very fact that the Party is no longer underground and is today extremely active in current society poses critical decisions for it.

For example, what position should the Party take toward black nationalism? What about the violence being perpetrated by extremist groups and individuals? The New Leftists are talking about "resistance" and "revolution." What does this mean to the Party?

Remember, in the New Look Party every effort is being made to be "respectable." Yet the Party now sees college students and black nationalists claiming to lead the nation to a new type of "revolution." Where does that leave the Party?

At this moment Hall is wrestling with these problems—giving him both challenges and tremendous opportunities.

The New Left

The "independent radical" newsweekly *Guardian,* carrying a news story from East Lansing, Michigan, about the 1968 convention of the New Leftist Students for a Democratic Society (SDS), commented:

> The new left in the United States has developed in the last several years from liberalism to anticapitalism, from reformism to revolution.
>
> Mistakenly defined by the old left as differentiated only by chronology and style, the new left is in the process of developing a sophisticated analysis of American capitalism and methods of revolutionary struggle.
>
> Students for a Democratic Society (SDS), the major organizational expression of the new left, evidenced as it met in convention here June 9–15 that such political development is accompanied by pain as well as promise.

Accompanying the article was a picture of a trio of New Leftists waving two flags. The caption read: THE RED AND THE BLACK: *Flags of Socialist Revolution and Libertarianism Fly Together at SDS Convention in Michigan Last Week.*

These two flags—the red of communism and the black of anarchism—reflect both the inner meaning of the student New Left movement and the dilemma of the Communist Party in its relations with this rapidly growing group.

In the New Left today we find a plethora of Marxist words and concepts (such as "imperialism," "class struggle," "capitalism," "revolutionary struggle"). Whether the New Leftists admit it or not, Marxist theory has deeply penetrated their thinking. Like the communists, the New Leftists denounce American "capitalism" and "imperialism," what they call the "Establishment." They detest (as do the communists) the military, law enforcement, and other Government agencies. They harass military recruiters on campus, heckle prominent Government officials, even physically threaten the safety of visitors at their schools.

The hard core of the New Left is the SDS. This group, for example, spearheaded the assault in the spring of 1968 against Columbia University, where students occupied buildings, kidnapped university personnel, and deliberately destroyed property.

At the SDS's 1968 convention, a workshop on sabotage and explosives was held. In this workshop, students discussed, for example, disrupting Selective Service and police facilities during riots, mailing letters dipped in combustible materials, firing Molotov cocktails from a shotgun, inserting "thermite bombs" in manholes to destroy communications.

In a piece of literature widely circulated by the New Left, actual instructions (with illustrations) are set out on how to prepare a Molotov cocktail and an incendiary time bomb. Listen to these words on how to use incendiary devices against induction centers:

Set to go off in the early morning hours (after 3:00 A.M. or so) such a device would do what the Oakland and New York demonstrations set out to do with several thousand people. It would not only close down the induction center—it would make the building itself useless for a period of weeks. There would, moreover, be no police violence and no mass arrests —but also no induction center.

This do-it-yourself manual of violence continues:

Needless to say, action against induction centers and local boards should not be restricted to "big" actions (such as delayed action incendiary devices) or nothing. Especially in smaller towns and villages, where many draft boards are relatively old frame structures and where police patrols are spotty, simple Molotov cocktails can be thrown through windows from side streets, resulting in the same extensive damage witnessed in Newark and in Detroit, but without the arrests. Furthermore, simply continually breaking windows and strewing parking lots with broken glass and bent carpet tacks are relatively minor but effective methods of harassing Selective Service employees. Likewise, any of a number of minor actions directed against the automobiles of draft board members (such as slashing tires, breaking windows, etc.) can be effective parts of a pattern which, as it becomes widespread, will spell first inconvenience, later harassment, but finally fear for all Americans who continue to act as tools of the Selective Service System.

In a recent article Tom Hayden, one of the founders of SDS, talked proudly of the New Left's "accomplishments" at the Columbia University riots. "American educators," he said, "are fond of telling their students that barricades are part of the romantic past, that social change today can only come about through the processes of negotiation. But the students at Columbia discovered that barricades are only the beginning of what they call 'bringing the war home.' . . . Create two, three, many Columbias," urged Hayden.

What is the future direction of the SDS and the New Left? The *Guardian* gives an interpretation based on the East Lansing convention:

> SDS, which in the last twelve months has evolved from an anti-imperialist to an anticapitalist perspective, is on the precipice of *embracing socialism or, in the terminology of a considerable number of SDS members, revolutionary communism.* (Italics added)

This is the red flag of communism—and the Party agrees with the New Left's detestation of "capitalism," the "Establishment," the draft, the war in Vietnam. These young people are actually mouthing opinions which the Party has long advocated.

But the Party does not like the other flag—the black flag of anarchism. Actually, SDS is anarchist and nihilist, urging destruction of the existing order but offering virtually nothing positive to replace it. Its members are largely undisciplined; they distrust people over the age of thirty and hate all kinds of bu reaucracies—including the bureaucracy (and discipline) of the Party.

In this chanting, aggressive, and amorphous group of students, the Party finds much to abhor. Hall, at the Party's special convention in July, 1968, denounced New Left concepts of revolution and guerrilla warfare as "petty bourgeois radicalism" and "antiworking class." Following *Pravda*'s lead, Hall singled out Professor Herbert Marcuse, philosophy professor at the University of California at San Diego, for special criticism. Here we come to the nub of communist disagreement with the New Left.

Ever since the days of Karl Marx and Mikhail Bakunin (the famous Russian anarchist), Marxists and anarchists have been enemies. As a Marxist, Hall dislikes the lack of discipline, the distrust of all authority, the blind destructiveness of anarchy. To his thinking, revolution must be channeled, harnessed, controlled— and this must be through the leadership and direction of the Communist Party. Hence, so-called guerrilla warfare and random acts of violence are wrong. Not that the communists disapprove in theory of violence, for Karl Marx said: "Force . . . is the midwife of every old society which is pregnant with the new." But anarchistic violence breeds the violence of the "capitalist state," thereby injuring the "true revolution."

However, according to Marcuse's teaching, the working class—the proletariat—which is the class Marx said would bring about the revolution, has lost its revolutionary fervor. Modern industrial democracy, Marcuse claims, has the ability to absorb and accommodate change without permitting any real and substantial change in society. A majority of the workers, especially those in the United States, have been bought off with a measure of prosperity, kept pacified by television and other mass media, and have become a prop of the Establishment. Hence, the working class is not revolutionary.

These concepts strike a strong blow at the theory of Marxism—and rile the Party.

Yet the Party today is working desperately to influence the New Left and young people. In 1964 it established the W.E.B. DuBois Clubs of America as a youth front. This group, named after a famous Negro educator, author, and leader who joined the Communist Party at the age of ninety-three, is the "fingers of the Party" on campuses. It has participated in anti-Vietnam war demonstrations, protests against Government officials, the staging of picket lines—doing all this in its effort to recruit young people. Approximately one-third of the Party's National Committee is considered as "youth" (that is, under the age of thirty-five).

From the New Left's agitation on campuses, the Party envisions an abundant harvest. The New Leftists have no hesitancy in working with communists and DuBois Club members. Here lies an immediate danger. How many of these young people, bitterly "anti-Establishment" in their thinking, will be captured by the superior discipline and organization of the Party? How many of these college students will be so caught up in their hatred of democracy and America that they will enter the ranks of Marxism-Leninism?

These new recruits will then drop the black flag of anarchism and raise the red flag of communism. Here is an area every concerned American should watch. The stakes are high.

The Civil Rights Movement and Black Nationalism

Like New Leftism, civil rights and black nationalism have presented both opportunities and problems for the Party.

Starting in the late 1950's, the Party stepped up its attempts to exploit the civil rights movement: assigning organizers to troubled racial areas, instructing members to participate in demonstrations, attempting to contact and influence prominent civil rights leaders.

As is to be expected, the Party posed—falsely—as the champion of the Negro people. It publicly championed civil rights legislation, the dismantling of Jim Crow laws, and the integration of public schools.

Yet despite this vocal championship, the Party's ability to recruit Negroes has basically been a failure. Roughly, only ten percent of the Party's membership is Negro, despite a disproportionate amount of time, money, and effort spent in this field. Historically, the Party has elevated Negro members to positions of ostensible leadership; for example, James W. Ford, nominated in 1932 for Vice-President of the United States on the Communist ticket. Benjamin J. Davis, Jr., now deceased, was long a top Party national official, while the current National Chairman (a figurehead position) is Henry Winston, a Negro. The Party's 1968 presidential candidate, Charlene Alexander Mitchell, is a Negro.

Recently, however, an illegitimate monster—black extremism—has arisen within the civil rights movement. How is the Party to deal with the increasing clamor, both inside its structure and in society as a whole, for extremist black power?

At the heart of this dilemma lies the Party's Marxist concept of the class struggle. Historically, the Negro has been regarded by the Party as part of the working class, which, it claims, is the revolutionary class. Hall, making his report to last July's Special Convention, re-emphasized this point:

"It is a system of special oppression of a people within a nation. The oppression is racial. The oppression is of a nationality. The oppressed by and large are of the working class. Being exploited at the point of production determines this class status for the great majority of black Americans. Thus the main economic issue is not land. The main economic issues are within the structure of U.S. capitalism. It is a special system of oppression interwoven into the fabric of capitalist exploitation."

In other words, the Party, again in Hall's words, wants to "speak about and for a working-class party uniting black and white."

This reasoning led to the modification at the 17th

National Convention (1959) of the Party's Moscow-directed concept from the 1920's that the Negroes in the United States were an "oppressed race" in the South struggling for "self-determination" and an oppressed national minority in other areas of the country struggling for equal rights. According to this concept, Negroes in the South had a right to set up a separate nation.

The Party's 1959 action discarded the concept of Negro "self-determination," and projected instead the idea that there should be Negro-white cooperation for the creation of a revolutionary working class. This action came in accordance with the then current Soviet policy of peaceful coexistence with the "imperialist powers." Moreover, there was the realization that the vast majority of Negroes in the South did not want a separate nation. "All signs point," said a position paper on the Negro question adopted at this convention, "to an early and triumphant resolution of the centuries-old battle of the Negro people for full and equal citizenship."

But based on the rise of black nationalism, the concept of the right to self-determination has again risen and is the subject of wide discussion in intra-Party circles. New factors have entered: the concept could now be applied to the North as well as the South. What does black power really mean? Moreover, some proponents advocate the use of force to achieve it.

The Party, not knowing which way to go, is groping:

Therefore, we have to ask: On the basis of present-day trends and currents, can we conclude that the Afro-American community is developing in the direction of a separate territory and a separate economy? I don't think the trends would sustain such a conclusion. It would be overdrawing on the separatist tendencies that do exist.

On the other hand:

While the *form* of the concept of self-determination does not apply to the present realities of black liberation, the spirit, the ideological essence, the essential political and moral quality behind the concept is present.

The Party's position, therefore, is one of "flexibility," meaning that it seeks to reap benefits from both sides: moderates and black power advocates. However, it can swing whichever way the future wind blows.

We can expect, based on past experience, that the Party will make every effort to assist those striving to create racial agitation and strife. The Party has always been quick to exploit unfortunate racial situations. The communists relish racial tensions and problems for the reason that they intensify the turmoil and troubles on which communism is nourished.

Claude Lightfoot, chairman of the Party's Negro Commission, provides an insight into the Party's real aim. Writing in a book, *Ghetto Rebellion to Black Liberation* (published in early 1968), he comments that the Party's present reluctance to support guerrilla warfare by Negroes in the ghettos is not based on the rejection of violence.

Rather, he says, the Party has never renounced force and violence per se; at certain times "armed struggle may be required." Lightfoot defends violent actions in the ghettos as "of a defensive nature," but notes that while it is one thing to defend oneself from attack by all necessary means, it is another thing to choose this way as the chief method. It is a matter of timing.

What could be more clear? In other words, violence is the historic communist approach to rebellion. It is wrong to rebel unless one can be assured the time is right. At this moment in history, in the Party's opinion, the time is not appropriate.

What about next month? Next year?

In black nationalism, as in New Leftism, the Party, despite open denials, is extremely sympathetic to the use of violence. However, it wants to determine how and when violence is to be used.

Labor and Industry—the Problem of the Stuffed Goose

"It is an epoch when the oppressed smell victory in the air," a Party leader commented. Unfortunately for the Party, the so-called "oppressed" working man in the United States doesn't know he is "oppressed"— at least in sufficiently large numbers.

Here is the Party's major problem in labor and industry. It still claims that the working man—the proletariat—is the class which, under the Party's guidance, will bring about the revolution. "Our Party is not a Party *for* the working class. Our Party is a working-class Party." Yet over fifty years after the revolution in the Soviet Union, the laboring man in this country still does not show much evidence of being revolutionary. Paradoxically, the major revolutionary base appears to be developing from New Leftists on the campus (which to Marx would have been an almost unbelievable base for a scientifically directed revolution).

In the 1930's and during World War II the Party achieved sizable influence in the labor movement. The union locals and some industrial union councils became sources of considerable Party power: contributing money, "fronting" for Party objectives, providing methods of infiltration. After 1945, however, much of this power was wiped out by the commendable house-cleaning efforts of the unions themselves.

But not entirely. Certain elements of American labor are still infiltrated. The problem of the Party, however, in this field is, in the words of Gus Hall, the problem of the "stuffed goose."

What is the problem of the "stuffed goose"?

The laboring man—the labor movement in the United States—is not revolutionary in the Marxist sense. That is, the increase in wages, the rise of the workers' standard of living, better employment conditions, the harmonious working of labor-capital negotiations—all of these, in the Party's view, have "stuffed the goose" of the working man. Why should he hate his employer? Why should he seek to overthrow the capitalist system? Why should he be interested in joining the Communist Party?

The rising affluence level—"a Christmas goose capitalism"—has negated Marx's historic teachings that wealth would accumulate in the hands of fewer and fewer people and that the masses would become increasingly poor, thereby generating class conflict.

The concept of the "stuffed goose" irritates the Party. "Such is the path of petty bourgeois radicalism . . . It is an antiworking class reactionary concept, sugar-coated by left phrases."

The Party, therefore, must vigorously struggle against the "wrong" policies of trade-union leadership, the "labor aristocracy," the idea that the working class is now bourgeois (middle class) and not revolutionary. It must drum up anticapitalist feeling, the idea that workers are underpaid, exploited, and oppressed.

Here is the measure of the Party's dilemma and frustration in our affluent society, but it is not giving up:

> More than anything else the working-class movement, our Party and the revolutionary movement need "doctorates" based on first-hand exploitation in a steel mill. We need communists with master's degrees in first-hand experience in the speed-up of an automobile factory. We need bachelor's degrees in automated coal-mining, in the attrition of a sweatshop in textile, machine-building or rubber . . .

A working-class Party above all else needs workers from the basic industries, from the mills, mines and factories, in its membership and leadership councils.

Trade-union conferences are being held to attempt to renew the Party's influence in this field, where, historically, communist infiltration has always been strong. The Party's approach is directed not only against the old-line unions (most of which, the communists would say, are guilty of the "stuffed goose" fallacy), but also toward the unorganized, the economically disenfranchised, the minority groups not yet able to benefit from the "Christmas goose" of an affluent capitalism.

This is why the Party so strongly supported the poor people's campaign in Washington, and continues to back the demands of American Indians and minority groups in ghettos, and of any other group unhappy and discontented for any reason. The Party hopes to stir up dissension and discord among these people, endeavoring to vindicate Marx's teaching that the working class is the weapon of revolution.

The prospects are that the Party has a fertile field. The basic answer to the communist threat in this area is to bring solutions (economic, political, social) to the problems of these groups in our society. In other words, let them share in the bounty of the "stuffed goose."

Support of the Soviet Union—and Its Problems

Top leaders from most of the communist world gathered in Moscow in November, 1967, for the fiftieth anniversary of the Bolshevik Revolution. On November 4, 1967, the Palace of Congresses in the Kremlin provided a glittering setting for a meeting of this elite of the international communist movement. Gus Hall, hailed as a conquering hero, addressed this gathering.

For Hall, it represented a personal victory for a Minnesota-born boy whose slavish devotion to a foreign ideology had brought him to the inner citadel of communism.

For the Communist Party, U.S.A., it meant the culmination of almost a half century (since its founding in 1919) of complete obedience and loyalty to the Soviet Union.

The National Committee of the Party issued a statement reaffirming its determination to work for "American-Soviet friendship" and the triumph of "socialism" in the United States. Hall, in his speech, bitterly denounced this country and extolled his masters.

The Party in the United States has, on all occasions, supported Soviet policy. Certain Kremlin moves, such as the Russo-German pact of 1939 and Khrushchev's anti-Stalin speech, had brought convulsion and shock to both membership and leadership. But those members who disagreed either left voluntarily or were purged. The Sino-Soviet conflict brought intra-Party dissent, and a small group, believing the Party should follow the more militant Red Chinese view, was expelled and later formed what was to become the Progressive Labor Party. This highly militant group is pro-Mao Tse-tung.

However, the main body of the Party has always remained obediently pro-Soviet. A basic characteristic of the post-Stalinist Party is its attempt to carry out the Kremlin's directions.

Hence, the Party has bitterly denounced American policy in Vietnam. It supported the Soviet position in that country's dispute with Czechoslovakia over the latter's liberalization policies. In early 1968 Hall participated in a summit meeting of communist parties in Budapest. At a press conference, Hall declared that United States "imperialism" was the central issue uniting the sixty-seven communist and workers' parties attending the conference. Hall added that the meeting had unanimously approved a proposal of the United States delegation that it send a message of sympathy and support to North Vietnam for its valiant stand against "American aggression."

A steady flow of communists from this country to the Soviet Union and other communist countries continues. Besides Hall, Henry Winston, James Jackson, and Albert Lima were members of the official Party delegation to the fiftieth-anniversary celebration in Moscow. National Committee member Louis Diskin (from Illinois) returned to the United States from an extended tour in the Soviet Union and the Mongolian People's Republic as a guest of the Mongolian People's Revolutionary Party. Anton Krchmarek, Chairman of the Ohio District, went to Moscow in the spring of 1968 to attend a symposium commemorating the 150th anniversary of the birth of Karl Marx. Following this, he traveled to East Germany to attend a similar type of symposium. Claude Lightfoot went to Havana, Cuba, by way of Europe, to attend a conference of the Organization of Latin American Solidarity. Herbert Aptheker made a well-publicized trip to North Vietnam.

In the 1920's a joke made Party rounds. "Why is the Party like the Brooklyn Bridge?" The answer: "Because it is suspended on cables." Today cables are not necessary for Moscow's instructions. The constant personal travel of Party officials to Moscow makes possible conferences with top officials, including Leonid Brezhnev.

This subservience, however, does cause trouble for the Party, both among its members and from the general public. A college student may ask a Party lecturer: "How can you be an independent, American party, as you claim, when you jump every time Moscow barks?"

Faced with this question, the hollowness of the Party's position becomes clear. The spokesman can rationalize, equivocate, and fabricate, but the alert student quickly perceives that Hall and his associates are, in fact, puppets of a foreign power. Any claim to "legitimacy," "respectability" and "independence" is abrogated.

These penetrating questions need to be asked more frequently of the Party.

The Arab-Israeli war of 1967, on the other hand,

brought to a boil the disparity which often develops between Soviet foreign policy (which is based on promoting Russian national interests) and the honest feelings and desires of many members of the Communist Party, U.S.A.

In this conflict, Russia supported the Arabs against Israel. As expected, the Party in this country slavishly followed this line and came out for the Arab powers. Instantaneously, dissent erupted from members of Jewish background. They denounced the Party's position and supported Israel, some even volunteering to donate money and blood.

The problem of anti-Semitism in Russia is a constantly festering sore in the Party. Moscow claims there is no anti-Semitism. But report after report tells of continuing anti-Jewish acts in Russia. What about this? What does the Communist Party, U.S.A., say?

The Party's position has been one of indecision, equivocation, and postponed discussion. A Jewish conference was held in late summer, 1968, but the issue is still a stinging scorpion.

The Soviet invasion of Czechoslovakia in August, 1968, brought new headaches to the Party. As expected, Hall immediately supported Moscow's actions, but a few Party leaders (as during the Soviet repression of Hungary in 1956) dissented. The Party's National Committee in September, 1968, however, backed the Soviet position. This is in line with the Party's historic support of the Kremlin.

This latest incident of Russian action on the international scene, designed to protect Moscow's own national interests, is giving Hall problems. For example, Hall and his cohorts have been promulgating the idea that, since Stalin, communism has "changed"—that it is becoming more democratic and liberal. How then can the brutal Soviet attack on a small nation—a "fraternal" socialist nation—be justified? Can not the Soviets allow even a small degree of personal freedom to a brother communist nation? Hall has long been exclaiming that communism will ultimately achieve state power in this country, utilizing our American traditions and policies. In fact, Hall says, each noncommunist nation will achieve communism through its own national forms. How can this be if the Soviet Union, a half century after the Bolshevik Revolution, cannot tolerate the ethnic variations of a small communist state which has long been one of its most faithful lackeys? How can this Soviet act of imperialism be sold to the American people?

Yet past experience indicates that communist leaders in this country are so attuned to the zigs and zags of the Party line that they will meet this challenge with the same degree of dialectical skill they have displayed in previous similar situations.

Whither the Party, or How to Increase Communism's Appeal

Have you ever stood at a distance and observed a pond or a large body of water? Initially, the surface may appear calm. Hardly a ripple can be noticed.

However, as you approach the water more closely, you realize that the first reaction was superficial. The water is in constant motion, with currents crossing and crisscrossing at rapid and unpredictable rates.

So the Communist Party. At a distance the Party seems highly monolithic, with some exceptions, such as the Arab-Israeli war. Gus Hall seems to be calling the tune with the direct support of Moscow (which he is). Yet close observation shows that the New Look Party is not a congealed mass, but betrays considerable diversity of opinion and conflict.

This diversity of opinion is not over loyalty to the Soviet Union, but *whither the Communist Party, U.S.A.?*

How can the Party be made more relevant to today's society? How can it best take advantage of the "chaotic issues of the day" to increase Party influence? Should the Party become more militant, à la Mao Tse-tung, or more broad-based and nationalist in approach (as John Gates urged in the late 1950's)? What about the young generation? Should young communists such as Michael Zagarell and Bettina Kurzweil, the twenty-four-year-old daughter of Herbert Aptheker, be advanced more rapidly to top Party positions? If so, are they too ideologically immature to make "correct" decisions? The Party has been accused of being too bureaucratic, old-fashioned, status-quo minded. Is this true? How best can the enthusiasm of the New Left be brought to aid the Party?

In other words, *the big debate in the Party today is on how to make communism more attractive, especially to young people.*

A vociferous wing of the Party feels that the New Look Party should become more militant, aggressive, dynamic, and revolutionary. To them, the Party has been too successful in being accepted as respectable. The result, they claim, is that the Party is too conservative and non-risky, even betraying some of the basic principles of Marxism-Leninism.

Historically, the Party has attracted the activist, the individual who thrives on covert, clandestine activities, a conspiratorial view of history, and sees an "enemy" which must be destroyed. This kind of individual has contributed enormously to some of communism's most impressive episodes.

Today, however, in line with the Party's policy of carrying out Russia's current program of peaceful coexistence, the activist type finds himself, in the words of one expert, "stranded on the dry sands of dullsville." He feels that today's communism is not sufficiently aggressive, and therefore is no longer attractive enough to arouse the enthusiasm of many young people, such as those of the New Left who, with their "anti-Establishment" viewpoint, should find the Party an answer to their problems. Only by moving to the left can the Party, they say, compete with the New Left, black nationalism, and revolutionary activist groups.

According to this school of thought, youth should

be promoted inside the Party more rapidly. The Party should emphasize strongly the "big R" approach (especially, they say, since "revolution" and alienation are more than ever being discussed in student and youth circles today) rather than the tactic of the "peaceful road," which often seems slow and makes the Party just like any other political group.

In other words, the New Look Party should have, this group contends, a more revolutionary, activist appeal. In this way, the Party would attract more support.

The other wing feels that to promote communism as militant and revolutionary is self-defeating in our democratic society—that it can only alienate the great masses of people who recoil from concepts of "revolution," "violence," and "ideology." These approaches in the past have isolated the Party from the mainstream of American life and characterized communists as "bomb throwers," "anarchists," and "dangerous characters." The whole trend of the post-Stalinist Party, they contend, is away from Marxist sectarianism.

The proponents of this idea would be slow to promote youth to high positions of leadership. Many of these young people, though full of vigor, are ideologically immature. They have not been thoroughly indoctrinated in Party theory—a process which takes time.

The Party, according to this view, should attempt to ally itself with noncommunist groups—to effect legislation, fight discrimination, attack problems in society. In this endeavor, the communists can make friends and influence people, build up confidences and

gain respectability. What the Party needs, if communism is to be made attractive, it is contended, is to continue its post-1960 program of attempting to gain legitimacy.

Ultimately, through this form of reasoning, the Party will be able to achieve major electoral successes. People, no longer fearing communism, will vote directly and unabashedly for Party candidates. They will read with interest Party statements, listen to Party speakers, and respect Party pronouncements. No longer then, it is claimed, will the Party be a strange, esoteric group off the mainstream of American life.

Which is correct?

Actually, this debate is nothing new. Rather, it is a modern echo of the famous dispute in 1945 between William Z. Foster (who advocated a strongly militant Cold War policy) and Earl Browder, the Kansas-born Party leader, who, during World War II, pursued a friendly, cooperative policy with capitalism. (Both policies, revealingly, were dictated by the needs of Soviet foreign policy.) Earlier, Jay Lovestone had been expelled from the Party for allegedly espousing "American exceptionalism"—that is, he viewed capitalism in this country as an "exception" to the workings of Marxist-Leninist laws. Later, John Gates was to advocate unsuccessfully a more broad-based Party, more independent of the Soviets, with a greater appeal to the people.

At the heart of the discussion is the determining of what the Party line is at the moment—one of the most dangerously slippery areas in the whole jungle of communism.

To be too revolutionary, too left wing, too far isolated from the people, is to commit the sin of "left-wing sectarianism." To be too conservative, too friendly with noncommunists and thus lose the distinctive nature of the Party's Marxism, is to commit the sin of "right-wing opportunism."

For Americans, the debate means simply this: the Party is endeavoring to find out which way is best suited at this moment to infiltrate and destroy our national institutions. The basic aim of both groups is the same. The debate is over the tactics.

From past experience, the enemy will not use either one or the other method: *he will use both, depending on time and circumstance.* Gus Hall, as the master tactician, is in the center, able to draw weapons from both camps.

THE FALLOUT OF COMMUNISM

In this nuclear age the word "fallout" has become common. In over fifty years of communism in America (there were communists in this country before the actual founding of the Party in September, 1919), what has its destructive fallout been to our society?

The quotations in this book show that a constant communist ideological cloud has floated above the American national scene all these years. The Party has been in continual existence. It has ebbed and flowed in strength, power, and influence. It has received aid and encouragement from the Soviet Union and in turn has aided that nation.

We must be scrupulously honest in our assessment of the communist poison which has dripped from this ideologically radioactive cloud. Great damage can be done by exaggerating the extent of communism, the influence it has exerted, where and how it has exacted injury. Nothing is more important for Americans than to be factual, intelligent, and rational in their analysis. We must not be affected by hysteria, emotionalism, and unreasonable fear.

The quotations in the second part of this book, I feel, will emphasize several basic points:

1) Communism means primarily a threat from the Soviet Union and its satellites (as well as Red China and other communist nations).

2) The Communist Party, U.S.A., the largest communist group in the country, has remained obediently loyal to Moscow. A person cannot be a communist and a loyal American at the same time.

3) Communism is a totalitarian philosophy which embraces all phases of human life: education, art, literature, the press, etc. It is all-encompassing.

4) In the United States, no indication is apparent that communism has changed even in the slightest from its historic Marxist-Leninist core

of a materialist atheistic conspiracy dedicated to overthrowing the institutions of our society. Communism is not, as some claim, becoming more democratic through the passage of time.

5) Communism employs different façades or tactical changes of clothes to conceal its inner core of revolution and assault against this country. At present the Party has a New Look, post-Stalinist style. This tactic is just as dangerous, if not more so, than the Stalinist Party.

6) Communism is depending in large measure on noncommunist hands to do its work. As a small minority, it seeks through deception to gain your support. Americans must beware lest the Party achieve support through deception, masquerade, and false promises.

7) Disrespect for law and order is a fundamental cornerstone of communist tactics. Charges of "police brutality," "illegal arrest," and "persecution" have long echoed in the Party press. These false communist charges, unfortunately, have been taken up by other groups whose basic purpose is to destroy law and order and to create chaos.

8) A half century of communism has done much to make both the Party and its ideology respectable among many elements in our society. Too many Americans are today becoming ideologically disarmed. Here lies one of the Party's major gains over five decades.

9) Communism has been able to implant much of its Marxist vocabulary into the rising New

Left, "anti-Establishment" movements which are appearing on our campuses. The legacy of communism in this country has been to implant distrust of free government, law and order, and the rational solution of conflicts. Marxist terms are regularly used and applied in New Leftist student circles.

10) At the heart of communism is the concept of violence. Despite Party protestations to the contrary, violence is the ultimate weapon of the communist kit of tactics. He who believes that the communists are peace-loving and have given up the "games of violence" is badly mistaken. The violence doctrines of communist theory and practice have undoubtedly influenced New Left and black nationalist thinking.

11) The concept of the *class struggle* remains at the heart of communist revolutionary propaganda and agitation. There has been no lessening of the communist effort to convert issues, such as the civil rights struggle, New Leftism, infiltration into labor and industry, into class struggles—in accordance with historic Marxist teachings. The Party has absolutely no interest in reforms or any activity which would strengthen the existing society.

12) In these fifty years many varieties of communism have arisen, some competitive and hostile to each other. But not one variety, be it Soviet or Red Chinese, Polish or Yugoslav, Castro or Albanian, is a genuine friend of the United States. The common denominator which unites

all these polycentric varieties is hostility to this
country.

WHAT YOU CAN DO

Communism has hurled us a mortal challenge. The response of Americans—and the response
of free men everywhere—will determine whether or
not freedom itself survives. Understanding what communism is and how it operates will help us to meet this
challenge.

1) *Know more about communism factually.* Like
   a disease, the symptoms and modes of operation of this enemy must be studied. Nothing
   takes the place of informed study and knowledge.

2) *Realize that to gain factual knowledge about
   communism takes time, patience, and effort.*
   Too many people think they can learn about
   communism in just a few hours or with a mini-
   mum of work. This is not true. Every citizen
   should be willing to take sufficient time to
   learn the basic principles of this ideology to
   enable him not only to identify its operations,
   but to do what he can to combat it. There is no
   easy, simple solution.

3) *The fight against communism is the responsibility of all.* The communists exploit our
   apathy, indifference, and unconcern.

4) *Communism must be fought within the demo-*

cratic structure of our society. Never must we employ any technique which smacks of vigilantism or extralegality.

5) *We must be extremely careful whom we call communists. We must be certain of our facts.* Great damage can be done by reckless accusations, false charges, and the spreading of false rumors.

6) *Citizens and organizations should not conduct their own investigations.* Any person or group having information about sabotage, espionage, or subversive activities should immediately furnish it to the FBI. The job of investigating is that of the FBI.

7) *We must have positive beliefs in the power of freedom and democracy to lead men to higher levels of personal dignity and strength.* Just to be against communism, without emphasizing the positive aspects of freedom, can lead to fear, hysteria, and misunderstanding.

8) *As citizens, we must work to eliminate those weaknesses in our society, such as poverty, discrimination, and disease, which enable the communists to pose as champions of reform.* A society that creatively tries to eradicate these evils makes the task of the Party difficult.

9) *Americans, young and adult, should know more about the basic traditions of America,* our history, our national heroes, our democratic traditions. A young person versed in the concepts of George Washington, Thomas Jefferson, and

Abraham Lincoln will not follow the siren calls of communist traitors.

10) *Basic in the fight against communism is a faith in things spiritual,* in a creative and loving God Who is interested in the universe He has brought into being. Here has always been the strength of America.

In these fifty years I have been constantly strengthened and encouraged by the support of our people—by men and women and young children for whom love of country is fundamental. It is these people across our nation who have stood up against the communist attack and made this a country where men can live as free and independent citizens.

I know—as long as we are willing to fight, suffer, and die for our ideals of freedom—that communism can never conquer.

2

Quotations

What Is Communism?

COMMUNISM—A DEFINITION

Communism claims to be a philosophy which explains the origin of man, his development, and his ultimate destiny. It confidently promises to bring about a world in which full equality, an abundance of the material benefits of life, and complete social justice will prevail. In short, communism claims to offer all things to all men by promising to cure all the world's ills and establishing a paradise on earth.

But there is a vast difference between what communists say communism is and what it actually is. Communism, as we know it today, represents nothing more than a totalitarian form of socialism.

* * *

Communism is many things: an economic system, a philosophy, a political creed, a psychological conditioning, an educational indoctrination, a directed way of life.

Masters of Deceit, page 8

Communism is a system of thought and action originated by Karl Marx and Friedrich Engels, developed
by V. I. Lenin, continued by Joseph Stalin and his successors. This system advocates, among other things: (1)
a materialistic explanation of the origin of man and
the universe; (2) a comprehensive economic interpretation of history centering about the class struggle; (3)
abolition of the noncommunist state, which is conceived to be an instrument of exploitation; (4) a revolutionary theory, method, and a flexible course of
action to overthrow the state and the capitalistic system; (5) a moral code based on utility; on nonsuper-
natural class concepts; (6) abolition of all religions;
(7) a world-wide communist revolution; and (8) a
world-wide communist society.

Ibid., pages 341-342

Communism (Marxism-Leninism) is the revolutionary,
materialistic ideology used by its adherents to justify
their efforts to seize power by any and all means for the
forcible establishment of a world-wide totalitarian
social order.

A Study of Communism, page 19

A FALSE IDEOLOGY

Communists have always claimed that
communism is a philosophy. A philosophy is a system
of thought which attempts to furnish the ultimate an-

swer to the reason for man's existence and man's relationship to this existence. By definition, it seeks
ultimate truth. Hence, every philosophy must continually question all premises, conclusions, judgments,
values, and principles. However, the validity of the
basic theoretical premises of communism cannot be
questioned by its adherents, for these premises must
be accepted as facts.

Communism does not permit an objective search
for truth. Communism tolerates only efforts to justify
the validity of its alleged "scientific" principles. The
current conflicting interpretations of Marxism by the
leading communist countries—the Soviet Union and
China—demonstrate that communism is not "scientific." Therefore, communism is not, and cannot be, a
philosophy in the strict sense of the word. It is, rather,
an ideology—an interpretation of nature, history, and
society which is developed with some logic from premises which are demonstrably false but which are not
open to question or criticism by its adherents.

* * *

The Fascists and Nazis were not the only menace to
our internal security. To their forces must be added
the American Communists with their godless, truthless, philosophy of life. They are against the America
our forefathers fought and died for; they are against
the established freedoms of America. They pose behind

a dozen fronts; they have endeavored to infiltrate practically every stratum of life.

Address at Annual Commencement Exercises, Holy Cross College, Worcester, Massachusetts, June 29, 1944

Communist strength is based on duplicity, hypocrisy, and sham. The Communists are masters of mirage, painters of brilliant Utopias. Their success, strange as it may sound, has been achieved, to a large extent, by making calumny respectable, deceit a virtue, and downright falsehoods the unimpeachable truth. Their false gods, clad in the shining armor of "truth," "justice" and "mercy," are today masquerading, with a surprising degree of success, as the legitimate ideals of democracy —a democracy, they say, which has failed miserably to nourish the spirit of man.

"Unmasking the Communist Masquerader," article in *The Educational Forum,* May, 1950

Communism is a many-faced monster endeavoring to gain the allegiance of our citizens. The Communist operates under a cloak of double talk and hypocrisy, always concealing his true intentions. He falsely appeals to the noblest of men's thoughts—proclaiming that he works in the interest of "peace," "justice," and "mercy." He promises all things to all men.

All too often the uncritical citizen accepts these exterior cries of Communism, being unable or unwilling to see through the outer veneer of hypocrisy into the inner core of deceit and terror. Communism is a way of life, embodying many types of appeals—economic, social, political, philosophical. The citizen must always be alert.

Interview of Mr. Hoover for *The Pilot*, Boston, Massachusetts, February 18, 1956

Communist philosophy is demonstrably false. Communist tactics—individual and mass terrorism, infiltration and subversion, the abrogation of treaties, to mention just a few—are abhorrent to the entire civilized world. Yet communism represents a massive effort to transform not only the world but human nature itself. It offers the dream of a world-wide society in which, it is claimed, there will be lasting peace and harmony. The appeal of this false promise proves that the power of a myth is still a factor to be reckoned with in human relations.

"Communist Illusion and Democratic Reality," December, 1959 (pamphlet)

The attractions of communism are countered by the fact that millions have abandoned the Communist movement in disgust. No one word can accurately describe the feelings of these people. If there were one such word, it would probably be *disillusionment.* That disillusionment is a common characteristic of former Communists should not be surprising. When communism is studied objectively from a philosophical, economic, political, or any other point of view, the theory and practices of communism are found to be basically false, impractical, and invalid. In other words, communism proves to be in fact an illusion.

A Study of Communism, page 12

The Party is today, in every possible way, attempting to camouflage its true communist identity. We must be alert to the double talk of communism. The Party wants to convince you, and other patriotic citizens, that it is a legitimate political party within our democratic traditions—which it is not. It wants to convince you that it is American in origin, and works for the best interests of our country.

Actually, the communists are desperately seeking to change their public image—to be accepted as legitimate elements of our society. Let's be careful. Remember that communists are not loyal to our democratic traditions. They come as wolves garbed in sheep's clothing. Despite what they say, in beguiling language, they hate and detest the United States. Their chief interest is not to build, to make a better Nation, but to wreck and destroy.

"A Statement on Communism," March 27, 1967 (pamphlet)

GOAL—WORLD DOMINATION

The ultimate objective of communism, made abundantly clear by its principles and by its strategy and tactics, is world domination. This entails the seizure of total power by any and all means on a world-wide scale by an elite minority group—the Communist Party.

Communist dogma holds that the triumph of communism is inevitable because it has already been determined by laws as immutable as those which govern the physical sciences. It is for this reason that communists regard themselves as "riding the wave of the future" toward their "rendezvous with destiny." Neither the communist target of world conquest nor the tactics employed to achieve it have fundamentally changed over the years, despite periodic lulls in international tensions.

The expansion of the Soviet Navy to a world-wide ranging fleet, the stockpiling of intercontinental missiles in the Soviet Union, and the development of atomic weapons in Communist China are obvious evidence that there has been no change in the communist goal of world domination.

* * *

The godless, truthless way of life that American Communists would force on America can mean only tyranny and oppression if they succeed. They are against the liberty which is America—they are for the license of their own. When they raise their false cry of unity, remember there can be no unity with the enemies of our way of life who are attempting to undermine our democratic institutions. The Fascist-minded tyrant whom we conquered on the battlefields is no different from the American Communistic corruptionist who now uses the tricks of the confidence man until his forces are sufficiently strong to rise with arms in revolt.

Address at International Association of Chiefs of Police, Annual Meeting, Miami Beach, Florida, December 10, 1945

This fact, horrible but true, emerges: Communism, a brutal, godless, materialistic way of life which would ruthlessly destroy the values and ideals we cherish, has made appalling advances. Within a generation Communism has catapulted from a small, militant underground coterie into a world-wide conspiracy, already embracing one third of the earth's population, and knocking, in most literal terms, on countless other doors. Communism is a deadly menace; a scourge which threatens the very existence of Western civilization. It has altered the orderly progress of history, deflected men's hopes for a better world—whether permanently or temporarily depends, in large measure, upon the people of America, upon you and me. We must win this battle, for the alternative to victory is the erasure of freedom, perhaps forever, from the parchment of time.

"Foe to Freedom," article in *The Elks Magazine*, October, 1950

The Fifth Column victories of the Nazis have been surpassed by the Fifth Column victories of the Communists. The blueprints and objectives of these Red Fascists have been proclaimed to the world with far more clarity than those of Hitler and his cohorts. Unfortunately, there are many seemingly well educated and intelligent people in our own country who have not yet awakened to the realization of the world-wide perils which are a potential threat to our own peace and security. The time has long since been upon us to face and carefully weigh the dangers which threaten our peace and security. There are still too many citizens who are prone to scoff and underestimate the Communist menace.

> Address at the 1954 Homecoming Banquet of Catholic University, Washington, D. C., November 13, 1954

It is an incontestable fact that our country, the symbol of the free world, is the ultimate, priceless goal of international communism. The leaders of international communism have vowed to achieve world domination. This cannot be until the Red flag is flown over the United States.

> "Message from the Director to All Law Enforcement Officials," *FBI Law Enforcement Bulletin*, March 1, 1960

Today communism encompasses one third of the world's peoples and one fourth of the earth's land surface. Make no mistake—the challenge is total—communism seeks to extirpate forever from the annals of history the ideals of our Western Judaic-Christian culture. If communism conquers, the world will be rolled back into a new age of paganistic barbarism.

> "Wholly Loyal," article in *Crusader*, June, 1961

Communism is dedicated, by ideology and practice, to complete domination of the world. Communism aims to destroy all other social orders and to communize the entire world.

Communism advances its cause regardless of any cost to and demand on the individual.

A Study of Communism, page 195

Nowhere is the hope for peace more sincere than in the hearts of all true Americans. But in our quest for peace, we must never lose sight of the well-documented fact that every Red leader from Marx and Engels through Khrushchev, Mao and the American communist spokesman Gus Hall is dedicated to an ideology which upholds world conquest as its ultimate goal.

Address at Catholic Youth Organization Convention,
New York, New York, November 16, 1963

America is face to face with an ideology—atheistic communism—which denies every ideal we uphold. The forces of this conspiracy have, in a relatively short time, expanded their rule. . . . And with untiring efforts they continue to unleash their weapons of terrorism, subversion and vicious propaganda in an attempt to ensnare every nation in a giant communist web.

"America's Ideals—Its Mark of Greatness," article
in *The Union Central Advocate*, 1965 issue

Today, we face the challenge of two international camps of communism which dominate nearly one third of the earth's people. One of these facetiously speaks of "peaceful coexistence" while loudly rattling the sword of nuclear destruction. The other—more boisterous and crude—profanely plays the part of a twentieth-century Genghis Khan.

Both are vehemently anti-American; and, despite widely dramatized differences, they continue to cast but one shadow across the earth. It is the shadow of death and destruction in Vietnam; the shadow of blackmail and intimidation in West Berlin; the shadow of subversion and guerrilla tactics in Latin America and other noncommunist regions of the world.

Remarks prepared for delivery before The Regional Conference on Crime Prevention of the Michigan State Bar, Rochester, Michigan, June 8, 1967

LIFE UNDER COMMUNISM

From a philosophical, economic, social, and political point of view, the theory and practices of communism are basically false, impractical, and invalid. Stripped of its deception, the illusion of communism stands exposed in all its naked brutality.

There is a vast difference between communist principles and communist tactics and between what communism promises and what it produces. Communists have expanded and built an empire at a cost in human misery and waste of human life that is almost beyond calculation. In addition, the Soviet Union has demonstrated that it will go to any lengths to retain

its empire. Witness the brutal suppression of the up-
rising in Hungary in the autumn of 1956 and the invasion of Czechoslovakia in August, 1968.

* * *

Communism is tyranny, naked, brutal and terrifying,
The Communist myth stripped of its beguiling and
ersatz clothes, is a wicked, foul, hateful story. The
individual, in Communist society, is a pawn, subject
to the whims of the ruling elite. Civil rights are nonexistent; concentration camps the symbol of justice;
terror the order of the day. Communism is cynically
immoral, an abject disillusionment—all the more so
because it professes to be the savior of mankind, the
architect of an alluring paradise where injustice, misery
and war will be abolished.

> "Unmasking the Communist Masquerader," article
> in *The Educational Forum*, May, 1950

Communism is more than an economic, political, social,
or philosophical doctrine. It is a way of life; a false,
materialistic "religion." It would strip man of his
belief in God, his heritage of freedom, his trust in love,
justice, and mercy. Under Communism, all would
become, as so many already have, twentieth-century
slaves.

> *Masters of Deceit*, page VI

In the name of ending the exploitation of the common
man, the communist hierarchy has developed into a

parasitic ruling class which has imposed a ruthless tyranny over millions. In the name of humanity, Communism suppresses the most elementary human values and robs the individual of his inherent dignity and worth. In what is pictured as a workers' paradise, slave labor is commonplace and the working man is denied the right to strike. In the regime which claims to have eliminated all discrimination, anti-Semitism is virtually official policy. The pretension that communism stands for national independence is flagrantly contradicted by the brutal suppressions of the uprisings in East Germany, Hungary, and Tibet.

> "Communist Illusion and Democratic Reality,"
> December, 1959 (pamphlet)

Communism represents everything abhorrent to the American ideal. Whenever it gains the ascendancy, it ushers in totalitarian dictatorship with its rigged elections, purges, slave labor camps, brutality and all-pervading fear. Yet this ultimate in enslavement, which by treason and trickery seeks to destroy this great Republic and force the United States of America to grovel under the absolute domination of a brutal philosophy of materialism, continues to portray itself as the ultimate good for mankind.

> "Communism and the Knowledge to Combat It!"
> article in *The Retired Officer Magazine*, January–
> February, 1962

Where communism promises abundance, the disillusioned see hunger. They see tyranny, although communism promises freedom. They see brutality, thought control, oppression and human degradation where communism promised liberation, justice, and the development of a new Communist man in a better society. They see inhuman exploitation, not only of men, but of entire nations by a movement which pledges to end the exploitation of man by his fellow man.

A Study of Communism, page 13

The tragic irony of this mid-twentieth century decade is the heart-rending dichotomy between the vaunted claims of Communism to exalt man and its actual relentless and perverse subjugation of him to inhuman tyranny, with millions of men, women, and children behind the Iron Curtain being encased in a Communist strait jacket of conformity, meaninglessness, and spiritual impotence, all in the name of making man the master of his fate!

"Storming the Skies: Christianity Encounters Communism," article in *Christianity Today*, December 21, 1962

In over a century of communism, starting with the Communist Manifesto in 1848, have we ever seen free elections in a communist-operated organization or state? Where have we seen communists honestly calling for free intellectual discussions and an independent search for the truth? Where have we seen freedom of speech, the press, religion in communist countries? Where under communism have we observed an independent judicial system, where the judges were not controlled by the ideological system? Where under communism can men and women live without fear of sudden arrest, where virtually every move is subject to inspection and control? . . .

The cold, jagged rocks of history—and the personal lives of millions of people—prove that these are mere pipe dreams of imagination. These hopes are snares which can only bring despair. It has been said that a leopard will not change its spots. It can be said that communism, despite the efforts of its apologists, will forever be based on the dagger, the assassin's bullet and the use of force. Coercion, not freedom, is its key; hatred, not love, its legacy; death, not life, its promise. Communism is the philosophy of the mailed fist. No amount of camouflage can long conceal this deadly fact.

"A Statement on Communism," March 27, 1967 (pamphlet)

EARLY RECOGNITION OF THE COMMUNIST DANGER IN AMERICA

In November, 1917, the Bolsheviks seized control in Russia, gaining state power for the first time. That control, today, has widened into a vast communist empire. The attack is still being pressed. International communism will never cease to instigate "wars of national liberation" until the whole world, including the United States, is under the red flag of communism.

The Communist Party, U.S.A., began in September, 1919, as a small, disorganized group of fanatics. Today it is a dedicated conspiratorial organization operating under modern conditions as an arm of revolution. America remains the primary target of international communism, as it has been for over fifty years. Delegates from sixty-seven communist parties at a consultative meeting in Budapest, Hungary, in February, 1968, had only unanimous approval for a motion by Gus Hall to send a warm message of support to North Vietnam against American "aggression."

* * *

Throughout the articles issued by the Russian Communist Party and in fact all Communist Parties, there is particular stress laid upon the uselessness of patriotism. One of the fundamental principles of communism is the international character of the same and consequently any advocation of communism in the United States is directly in violation of the principles upon which this government was founded; namely, that of nationalistic sectionalism. With the existence of communism, patriotism disappears and the Utopian idea of the Communist is for one great international proletarian State.

> Brief prepared by J. Edgar Hoover on Ludwig Christian Alexander Kaslovitch Martens for the Attorney General of the United States, December 29, 1919, page 11

The essence of the communist program is that the proletariat must be so directed and educated that by mass action they will at one sweep destroy the State and establish a dictatorship of the proletariat in the form of soviets, which will exist until the bourgeois is suppressed and destroyed, and the proletariat is organized into the working groups and the communist commonwealth is established. They will only use parliamentary action (the ballot) as propaganda. . . .

. . . we see that not only is the Communist Party of America pledged to overthrow the Government of the United States by force and violence, but that it is also pledged to foment industrial unrest through mass strikes and to stir up and agitate racial prejudices throughout the entire country. . . .

From the examination of . . . the manifesto of the Communist International and the manifesto of the Communist Party of America, we find advocation of doctrines for the overthrow of the Government of the United States, not by parliamentary action but by direct action or mass action, which, as above shown, means force and violence. . . . However, in order that there may be no doubt as to the responsibility of individual members of the Communist Party of America, we have but to examine the application for membership which each member must sign upon entering the organization. The following is a statement taken from the application: "The undersigned, after having read the constitution and program of the Communist Party, declares his adherence to the principles and tactics of that party and the Communist International; agrees to submit to the discipline of the Party as stated in its constitution; and pledges himself to engage actively in its work."

Thus we see from the above that each and every member accepted for membership in the Communist Party pledges himself not only to the constitution and program of that party, but also to the principles and tactics of the Communist International, and further pledges himself to engage actively in the work of carrying out such principles and tactics.

> Brief on the Communist Party, prepared by J. Edgar Hoover, included in Hearings before the Committee on Rules, House of Representatives, Sixty-sixth Congress, Second Session, 1920, pages 326, 328, 329, 330

The communists do not intend, if we accept the meaning of their own language, to achieve the revolution with the authority of the existing government, by use of the ballot; but intend to achieve the social revolution by ruthless infliction of the ideas of a small minority upon the will of a majority, to be accomplished by force and violence. This is literally, "eternal anarchy amidst the noise of endless wars," and if it be not a doctrine that organized government should be overthrown by force or violence or by unlawful means, then language has lost its force and words are meaningless. The ignorant primarily, but also the vicious, criminal element, which in Russia has murdered all who stood in their way and has robbed all who had any wealth, have accepted the doctrines of communism. No right-minded person can countenance such revolutionary propaganda as the communists are spreading. It is not their sincere purpose to better the condition of the workingman or to improve the economic or social life of this country; but their purpose is political, as stated; political in that their objective is the overthrow of the political state. . . .

The principles of Communism, as enunciated by the leaders of the European movement, find expression in toto in the doctrines of the Communist Labor Party of America. These doctrines threaten the happiness of the community, the safety of every individual, and the continuance of every home and fireside. They would destroy the peace of the country and thrust it into a condition of anarchy and lawlessness and immorality that passes imagination.

> Brief on the Communist Labor Party, prepared by J. Edgar Hoover, included in Hearings before the Committee on Rules, House of Representatives, Sixty-sixth Congress, Second Session, 1920, pages 153, 154

COMMUNIST PARTY, U.S.A.— FAITHFUL TO MARXISM-LENINISM

According to communist ideology, the Marxist science of the laws of social development enables communists not only to chart a correct path through the labyrinth of social change, but to predict the course events will take, the direction of historical progress, and the next stage of social development. Thus, Marxism-Leninism supposedly gives communists an instrument with which to look into the future and see the outlines of impending historical changes.

A draft of a new program, published by the Communist Party, U.S.A., in March, 1968, states that the Party's world outlook is "scientific socialism," or Marxism-Leninism. The document describes Marxism-Leninism as the science of social change and says: "It is revolutionary because central in its conception is the historical reality that the climactic point of social change, the replacement of one social system by another, is a revolutionary act."

The Communist Party, U.S.A., continually emphasizes the correctness of Marxism-Leninism and the need for Party members to accept these tenets as a guide to thought and action. Even in times of unusual circumstances, such as the period of underground activities by the Communist Party, U.S.A., in the early 1950's, the Party is the sole interpreter of the doctrine of Marxism-Leninism.

*   *   *

The communist movement in the United States began to manifest itself in 1919. Since then it has changed its name and its party line whenever expedient. But always it comes back to fundamentals and bills itself as the party of "Marxism-Leninism." As such, it stands for the destruction of our American form of government; it stands for the destruction of American democracy; it stands for the destruction of free enterprise; and it stands for the creation of a "Soviet of the United States" and ultimate *world* revolution.

"Communism in the United States," article in *Confidential—from Washington*, June, 1948

The members have been conditioned, during the past few years, to act on their own by applying the fundamentals of Marxism-Leninism to the problem at hand. Membership records no longer exist. Communist Party clubs, which at one time would number a hundred people, have been broken down into groups which have only three to five members today. The very actions of the individuals give a pretty clear picture of the fact that they don't want to be out in the open. They're sending couriers from district to district, and by word of mouth are passing out party orders.

"Communist Threat in U.S.," article in *U. S. News and World Report*, March 30, 1951

Those who now remain in the Communist Party are essentially the real nucleus of hard-core communists who are devoted to Marxism-Leninism and are willing to obey any party instructions.

"Where Do We Stand Today with Communism in the United States?" article in *The American Legion Magazine*, March, 1954

Party members vehemently uphold the tenets of Marxism-Leninism. To them, the communist philosophy is "a guide to action," a doctrine which they believe will direct them toward the goal of communism in the United States.

"The Communist Party, USA," article in *Social Order*, September, 1961

The Communist Party, U.S.A., for tactical reasons, attempts to camouflage its atheistic convictions. However, it is a faithful champion of the atheism of Marx, Engels, Lenin and Khrushchev and is working today to undermine the religious faith of the American people.

"Let's Fight Communism Sanely!" article in *Christian Herald*, January, 1962

The Communist Party, USA, realizes that if it is to accomplish its historic role it must constantly train new leadership and indoctrinate the membership in Marxism-Leninism. In furthering the Marxist education of its members, the party is stressing the study of the manual, "Fundamentals of Marxism-Leninism," published by the Foreign Languages Publishing House in Moscow. Communist statements for public consumption to the contrary, the material furnished for study within the party clearly reveals that the use of force and violence is—as it has always been—the technique for the Communist seizure of power. For, "Fundamentals of Marxism-Leninism" specifically states: "The highest stage of the proletariat's class struggle is revolution."

A Study of Communism, page 167

The Party then is more than a study group, a research organization, or a discussion club—it has for its basic purpose revolutionary action based on the "scientific laws" laid down by Marx and Engels. Moreover, this revolutionary action must be under Party control, not individually conceived and executed forays.

> Statement by Mr. Hoover concerning the 18th National Convention, Communist Party, U.S.A., June 22–26, 1966, published by the Senate Internal Security Subcommittee

COMMUNIST PARTY, U.S.A.—ALLEGIANCE TO SOVIET UNION

The policies, programs, and activities of the Communist Party, U.S.A., from 1919 to the present show that it has consistently supported those of the Soviet Union. It has continued on a virtual day-to-day basis to justify all the policies and actions of the USSR and to exert every effort to defeat or negate the policies and activities of the United States which run counter to those of the Soviet Union.

Typical was the attitude of the communist newspaper, the *Daily World*, during the summer of 1968, when the Soviet-bloc countries were still threatening military intervention to halt a liberalization trend in Czechoslovakia. In an editorial in its July 26, 1968, issue, it was stated that close examination revealed that the "so-called conflict" between the communist leadership of Czechoslovakia and the communist leaders of the Soviet Union, Poland, East Germany, Bulgaria, and Hungary was a " 'conflict' manufactured in political and press circles of the imperialist countries, mainly the U.S."

Following the military intervention in Czechoslovakia by the Soviet Union and its allies in August, 1968, General Secretary Gus Hall released a personal statement in which he parroted Soviet justification of this action by claiming that there was a threat of counterrevolution in Czechoslovakia. Hall said that it would be a "fatal error" to underestimate the danger of an "antisocialist takeover."

The Communist Party, U.S.A., has categorically denounced all the policies and programs which our nation has adopted since World War II to defend ourselves and our allies against the threat of further communist aggression. These include the Marshall Plan, the North Atlantic Treaty Organization, aid to Greece, United Nations intervention in Korea, and American involvement in the Vietnam war.

* * *

The Communist Party in the United States is a faithful adherent of the Moscow line. When the Kremlin trumpet sounds, the American stooges echo and re-echo the tune. They make worshipful obedience to the Master on High. If, by chance, they make a false step, and sound the wrong tune, they must recant—a grave error, an unpardonable breach of discipline which cannot be tolerated. Not only must this error never be committed again but the erring comrade must be "re-educated," which means, in Communist terminology, that the Party members must be better indoctrinated, especially in the art of agility, of landing at all times on the platform of the current party line.

> "Foe to Freedom," article in *The Elks Magazine*, October, 1950

The record speaks for itself. The Communist Party in the United States from its inception has never deviated from the Moscow line.

> "Communist Threat in U. S.," article in *U. S. News and World Report*, March 30, 1951

For the alert and thinking citizen, no cloak of camouflage can conceal the fact that the Communist Party, USA—in the past, present, and future—is the willing tool of the Moscow masters of deceit.

> "Message from the Director to All Law Enforcement Officials," *FBI Law Enforcement Bulletin*, April 1, 1959

The Communist Party, USA, as an integral part of the international communist movement, represents a beachhead of subversion within our own Nation. So long as the communist movement threatens to impose its domination on the entire world, the Party will represent a threat to our internal security. Consciously

modeled after the Communist Party of the Soviet
Union, the Communist Party, USA, is today a tightly
knit, hard-core group which offers its unswerving allegiance to the Soviet Union. In the showdown with
the United States which the communists insist is inevitable, there is no doubt that the Soviet Union is
relying heavily on the Party as an advance detachment
within our borders ready and willing to carry out any
hostile act within its capability.

"Communist Illusion and Democratic Reality,"
December, 1959 (pamphlet)

In the United States, the international communist
movement is represented by the Communist Party,
USA. As the history of the communist movement in
the United States proves, the Communist Party, USA,
has been inspired and completely controlled by the
fountainhead of world communism, the Soviet Union.
Every major phase of the Party's historical development has been determined, not by any factor indigenous to the United States, but rather by the exigencies
of communist imperialism.

"One Nation's Response to Communism," September, 1960 (pamphlet)

The entire history of the Communist Party, USA,
demonstrates conclusively that it has selected its leaders, formulated its policies, and shifted its tactics,
either on the basis of specific Soviet directives, or as a
reflex response to Soviet action. To this day, the Com-

munists in the United States pledge their allegiance to the Soviet Union.

A Study of Communism, pages 159–160

Here in the United States, the cause of international communism is represented by the Communist Party, USA—a cunning and defiant subversive conspiracy which is financed, directed and controlled by the Kremlin. Its membership consists today of a hard core of revolutionary fanatics who are knowingly and eagerly subservient to the dictates of Moscow. The dupes, the dissidents and the faint of heart have long since been purged from the Party's ranks.

Address at Brotherhood of the Washington Hebrew
Congregation, Washington, D. C., December 4, 1963

No action of the Soviet Union—regardless of how reprehensible—draws the reproach of Communists here. Rather, the Party consistently heralds Russia as a harbinger of "peace" and "progress."

"America's Ideals—Its Mark of Greatness," article
in *The Union Central Advocate,* 1965 issue

Since 1919, when it was organized, the Communist Party, U.S.A., has formulated its policies and altered its tactics either on the basis of specific Soviet instructions or as the result of an almost conditioned response in defense of the Soviet Union—the party's only reason for existence.

The Communist Party, U.S.A., in line with instructions from the Soviets, has made every effort to obstruct all measures which our Nation has taken to defend itself and to strengthen our allies against the threat of further Communist expansion. The Party has opposed practically all military, economic and political agreements which we have made with other non-Communist nations throughout the world. At the same time, the Party has defended such aggressive Communist actions as the Communist takeover in China and the European satellite nations and the brutal suppression of the uprisings in East Germany and Hungary.

1966 FBI Appropriation Testimony, page 54

Inside the United States there is today an aggressive, bold and highly confident Communist Party. Organized in 1919 at a convention in Chicago, Illinois, the Party has always been obediently loyal to Moscow. At this moment, its officers and members, along with thousands of sympathizers or "state of mind members," form a phalanx of treason in our midst. The Party is working in every possible way to infiltrate, subvert and destroy our democratic form of government.

"A Statement on Communism," March 27, 1967 (pamphlet)

Make no mistake about the communists in this country. They represent a conspiracy of international treachery and deceit—one which is totally and unapologetically subservient to the dictates of Moscow.

Remarks prepared for delivery before The Regional Conference on Crime Prevention of the Michigan State Bar, Rochester, Michigan, June 8, 1967

Although the party in this country protests that it is independent of the Soviet Union, the unending stream of party functionaries and delegations traveling to Moscow shows that the party remains—as it always has been—an obedient slave to its Soviet masters.

The determination of the Soviet Union to maintain the Communist Party—U.S.A. and to strengthen and direct it in such a way as to make it a continuing danger to this Nation is clearly evidenced by the fact that for the past 47 years Soviet Russia has in one way or another directed and controlled the Communist Party—U.S.A. and helped to finance it.

1968 FBI Appropriation Testimony, page 44

How Communism Works

COMMUNISM AND RELIGION

Communists completely reject a belief in God, in morals derived from religious principles, and in the immortality of the soul. Communism is based on dialectical and historical materialism, which arbitrarily excludes all convictions based on faith in God and the theistic interpretation of life.

Communism simply cannot tolerate freedom of religion and all that it signifies. No communist government can permit allegiance to any authority but its own, whether that authority be a Supreme Being, a code of ethics, a body of political and social principles, or merely an individual's respect for his own mind and conscience. To tolerate two authorities would lead to a freedom of choice for citizens, and citizens who are free to choose would be unreliable by communist standards.

Communists in the United States soft-pedal their antireligious sentiments as a tactical maneuver in order to depict an ostensible mutuality of interests and agreement with religion on such issues as peace, civil liberties, civil rights, and social welfare. In an article written for publication in July, 1968, for example, Gus Hall said, "Our fight is not with God. It's with capitalism and all that capitalism has done to oppress people."

* * *

The danger of Communism in America lies not in the fact that it is a political philosophy but in the awesome fact that it is a materialistic religion, inflaming in its adherents a destructive fanaticism. Communism is secularism on the march. It is a mortal foe of Christianity. Either it will survive or Christianity will triumph because in this land of ours the two cannot live side by side.

Lecture prepared for delivery at the Conference of Methodist Ministers, Garrett Institute, Evanston, Illinois, November 26, 1947

The godless tyranny of atheistic Communism has recognized that it cannot survive alongside a religion that changes men's hearts—because what it teaches as truth pales to extinction when placed before the truth of God's way. That is why Communists are taught that religion is the opiate of the people; that is why the Communists scoff at the Life Everlasting; that is why, when the strategy and tactics of Communism are revealed, they stand revealed as a foe of God. Communism means godlessness. Godlessness means slavery.

Slavery means spiritual and physical death. The definition of Communism is as simple as that.

Remarks before the Military Chaplains Association
of the United States, Washington, D. C., May 5, 1954

Why does the Church—which has no military forces—merit the most explosive of Communist rockets, the most venomous of Communist hate, the most vituperative of Communist scorn? Because religion, of all facets of Western civilization, represents the eternal "thorn in the flesh" of communism, that jagged rock which is constantly puncturing, exposing, and unmasking Communist claims, performances, and hopes. The Communists realize that unless the Christian pulpit—that mighty fortress of God—is liquidated, pitilessly, mercilessly, finally, the very existence of communism itself stands in jeopardy. The spiritual firepower of the Christian Church—based on the love of God—is sufficient to destroy all the Soviet man-made missiles and rockets and extirpate this twentieth century aberration.

And the Communists know it—and fear it.

"Communist Propaganda and the Christian Pulpit,"
article in *Christianity Today*, October 24, 1960

Over the years, as could be expected, churches and religious organizations have been—and will so remain—targets for communist infiltration. In the past, some clergymen, unfortunately, have been drawn into the communist movement. But the overwhelming majority of our clergymen are today wholly loyal to our nation and are working valiantly to protect our freedoms. This is not the time for name calling, for unfounded accusations or publicity-seeking charges designed to confuse, divide and weaken.

"Wholly Loyal," article in Crusader, June, 1961

To say merely that communism is atheistic is to set forth only part of the story. Communism and religion are diametrically opposed. Communism is religion's deadliest enemy. . . .

Communism holds that all religions are false and harmful and must be destroyed. It teaches that religion originated in superstition and later was used as an instrument to control and exploit the masses. Communism holds that religion can have no place in the communist social order and that all religions must be ruthlessly destroyed.

"The Deadly Contest," article in Columbia magazine, August, 1961

Over all, the Party has not had marked success in its attacks against the church. The Communists have found in religion a foe of the greatest tenacity, able to withstand the withering firepower of Marxist-Leninist chicanery. The overwhelming majority of America's clergy are loyal citizens, devoted to working for the best interests of the nation. Being men of God, they realize that Communism and religion are irreconcilable, that never can there be a truce between them.

"Let's Fight Communism Sanely!" article in Christian Herald, January, 1962

Communism strives to destroy religion in order to create the dehumanized "Communist man."

A Study of Communism, page 202

Yet despite this tremendous energy and this monstrous capacity to enslave men's minds, hearts, and souls, Communism is inherently weak when compared with the explosive power of man's urge to be free. This basic fact Americans so often overlook—that it is in the faith of our fathers, a trust in God, and a belief in the dignity of man that the real revolutionary power of history arises; and that it is this power that over the centuries has ripped apart tyrannies, overthrown dictators, and humbled the idolatrous.

"The Faith of Our Fathers," article in *Christianity Today*, September 11, 1964

MORALITY AND ETHICS

Communist morality is rooted in a total renunciation of a belief in God and the values of the Judaeo-Christian moral code. Communists subordinate all morality to the class struggle. To them, anything is moral which is related to the revolutionary struggle and which tends to destroy the enemy and to promote communism.

In their drive for power, communists are not inhibited by any legal, moral, or ethical scruples. Any action—legal or illegal, moral or immoral, peaceful or violent, open or secret—is justified if it advances the cause of communism. Communists never hesitate to use such means as force, terror, arrests, and mass murders to promote and to gain communist objectives.

In their public appearances in the United States, communists answer questions from the audience by giving half-truths, by lying, or by avoiding the question and resorting to a condemnation of the United States.

For example, Benjamin Dobbs, who was introduced as a person who joined the Communist Party in 1932, appeared on a TV program in Los Angeles in June, 1968. During his remarks Dobbs said that the Communist Party, U.S.A., is "an independent Communist Party that makes its own decisions." Dobbs was asked if the Communist Party independently decided that the war in Europe was of no concern to the United States as long as Hitler and Stalin were dividing Poland, and then independently decided that the United States should enter the war when Hitler attacked Russia. Dobbs replied to the effect that independence does not mean freedom from human error and that these decisions were influenced by the Party's opposition to war as a solution for issues.

* * *

But Communists do not mean what they say when they are speaking for public consumption. . . . The great god of the American Communists, Comrade Lenin, urged the use of deceit and trickery. His writings, which are their Bible, declare, "The strictest loyalty to the ideas of Communism must be combined with the ability to make all necessary practical compromises, to maneuver, to make agreements, zig-zags, retreats, and so on. . . .

Radio interview of Mr. Hoover on communism and subversive activities, February 15, 1948

Communism is immoral. The Communist teaches that the end justifies the means. . . .
    Communism lives on lies. It corrodes honor, destroys integrity, and subverts all the qualities which combine in an individual to make him, in the truest sense, a man.

"Communism and the College Student," article in Boston University *Campus,* March, 1953

Every communist unhesitatingly sacrifices his personal life to advance the cause of communism. He is not bound by any of the traditional moral or ethical scruples. Any action—violent or peaceful, lawful or unlawful, moral or immoral, open or covert—which will promote communist goals, automatically becomes justified.

"Communist Illusion and Democratic Reality," December, 1959 (pamphlet)

Hence, there arises the ugly manifestation of Communist "ethics"—namely, the Communist belief that morality must be subordinated to the class struggle, the inevitable conflict between communism and its opponents. What is moral? Anything which serves to destroy the enemy and promote communism. Lenin was most explicit: "Morality is that which serves to destroy the old exploiting society and to unite all the toilers around the proletariat, which is creating a new Communist society."

"The Communist Menace: Red Goals and Christian Ideals," article in *Christianity Today*, October 10, 1960

No communist must ever be permitted to allow compassion for others to deter him from carrying out communist objectives. Morality to the communists is merely expediency. In the words of Lenin, "We repudiate all morality that is taken outside of human, class concepts. . . . We say that our morality is entirely subordinated to the interests of the class struggle. . . ." In the name of communism, lies, trickery, terror—even murder—are justifiable. Such acts are right or wrong depending upon whether they help or hinder the cause.

"The Communist Party, USA," article in *Social Order*, September, 1961

Communist morality is highly flexible. It is based on a single premise—anything that promotes progress toward communism is necessarily good, and anything that interferes with that progress is necessarily bad. Communists call this standard of morality "proletarian utility." Convinced that capitalism is evil, Communists say they are morally justified in using any and all means to bring about its destruction and to establish in its place a world-wide Communist society. Communists completely reject not only the traditional Judaeo-Christian concept of morality, with its objective standards of what is right and what is wrong, but also the very idea itself that there can be any objective standard of morality. By the standards of Communist morality, nothing is absolute, final, or sacred—except communism itself.

A Study of Communism, pages 48–49

It is one of the glaring contradictions of our day that the same communist spokesmen who are so glib-tongued in their appearances before groups of college students immediately lose their voices when placed under oath in a court of law or before a Committee of Congress. They always take refuge behind the Fifth Amendment. Our moral atmosphere would be better if they knew as much about the Ten Commandments as they do about the Fifth Amendment.

Communists refuse to testify at *any* proceeding where they are subject to fines and imprisonment for deliberate lies and distortions. In the dark world of communism, there is no room for truth—just as there is no place for freedom and decency and God.

Remarks before the Supreme Council 33°, of the Ancient and Accepted Scottish Rite of Freemasonry, Washington, D.C., October 19, 1965

TREACHERY AND DECEIT

Chicanery, intrigue, and treachery are the stock in trade of communists, not only in dealing with their enemies but also in their relations with each other. These are the natural attributes of their Machiavellian system.

Deceit and perfidy govern all communist tactics and practices. Communists will resort to all sorts of stratagems, maneuvers, illegal methods, evasion, and subterfuge to gain their ends. The strictest loyalty to communist ideas is combined with the ability to make all necessary compromises, zigzags, and retreats.

Aesopian language or double talk is a prominent deceptive device used by communists to fool noncommunists. Communist Aesopian language always has two sides—the deceptive line for public consumption and the real Party line to advance communism. Hence, the words and terms uttered by communists, such as democracy and peaceful coexistence, have a meaning vastly different from accepted usage.

* * *

Many of the Communist Party's leaders stand convicted, in courts and in the public mind, of falsehood and deceit, but they are still on the march, burrowing deeper and deeper into our system of democracy.

There is a sneer behind their every smile and a vicious lie in their every promise of Utopia. If the land

whose banners they carry is Utopia, then let them go
there and enjoy it! America is good enough for us
and we do not want it tainted by the poisons of foreign
isms.

Address before the Drake University Commencement
Exercises, Des Moines, Iowa, June 3, 1940

We must all realize that the Red conspirators in our
midst still constitute a very grave menace. They continue to wage a relentless campaign to pervert our
thinking and undermine our freedoms. Their princi-
pal weapons are deceit, stealth, sham, and trickery. To
defeat them, we must recognize them as diabolically
skillful enemies, understand their methods, and be
eternally vigilant.

"The Communists Are After Our Minds," article in
The American Magazine, October, 1954

Make no mistake about it, the struggle ahead is real.
The Communists are determined, rugged, and treach-
erous enemies. The ideology of communism, as we
have seen, generates great power. But the faith of communism is a perverted faith, giving predominance to
evil, sin, and wrong. It draws its strength from deceit,
chicanery, and hypocrisy. That is its fatal flaw, the
rotten core which spoils the fruit of its branches.

"Soviet Rule or Christian Renewal?" article in
Christianity Today, November 7, 1960

The history of the modern Communist movement is
a chronicle of treachery and deceit. The pages of that

history abound with examples of individual and mass terrorism, broken treaties, infiltration and subversion of non-Communist governments and organizations, full-scale and guerrilla warfare, sabotage, genocide, repression of minorities, purges, assassinations, slave-labor camps, suppression of religion, the abrogation of individual liberty, and nuclear blackmail. Such are the tactics used by Communists as part of the over-all strategy through which they ultimately hope to communize the world.

A Study of Communism, page 76

Never before in its almost 50-year history in this country has the Party reached more of our citizens with its message of hate, bigotry and deceit.

Remember that a communist speaking on the radio, television or elsewhere is still a communist. His words are tailored to deceive, mislead and hoodwink. His melodious tune is designed to stifle independent thought, the intellectual search for truth. His whole aim is to destroy the very freedom of speech which he so falsely claims to uphold.

"A Statement on Communism," March 27, 1967 (pamphlet)

ATTITUDE TOWARD LAW

In a communist society, law and justice are designed and applied to maintain the omnipotence of the state, to which the individual is completely subservient. The interests of the communist state are pre-eminent and, therefore, take precedence over those of the individual. To communists, law is, by its very nature, inseparable from the state.

Communists recognize that they cannot infiltrate and undermine American society unless they first turn the people against established authority. To accomplish this, they try to influence and turn people against law and order and to smear and discredit constituted authority. For years communists have charged that legal proceedings which they oppose are "frameups" and that law enforcement officers are guilty of "police brutality" and "gestapo-like tactics." In particular, communists strive to arouse Negro hostility toward policemen as a means of fomenting racial strife.

* * *

I do say, however, that the Communist charge that there is the slightest desire in the FBI for an Ogpu or a Gestapo is nothing but blustering ballyhoo designed to cover their own "Trojan Horse" activities. The Communists hope that with the FBI shackled, they can proceed without interference as they go their boring, undermining way to overthrow our Government.

. . . These totalitarian tricksters are the very first ones who would introduce un-American, violent, murderous types of spy systems into our country. They desire to break down true law enforcement in every part of America under the guise of the protection of

alleged civil liberties so that they may, in turn, destroy
the very things that they pretend to revere.

Address before the New York Federation of
Women's Clubs, New York, New York, May 3, 1940

To the Fascist foe must be added another, the American Communist. These panderers of diabolic distrust
already are concentrating their efforts to confuse and
divide by applying the Fascist smear to progressive
police departments, the FBI and other American institutions to conceal their own sinister purposes.

Address at International Association of Chiefs of
Police Annual Meeting, Miami Beach, Florida,
December 10, 1945

Law enforcement has long been a target of communist
attack. As legal opposition crystallized, these Party
attacks, especially on the FBI, prosecutive officials, and
police, have mounted in intensity.

Lenin taught that it was essential for every "real
people's revolution" to destroy the "ready-made state
machinery." Wherever communists have been able to
exercise any measure of control, their first step has
been to hamstring and incapacitate law enforcement.

Masters of Deceit, page 210

Defiance of the law and outspoken disrespect for authority dominate the words and deeds of these un-
American conspirators.

Remarks at the Annual Conference, International
Association of Chiefs of Police, Washington, D.C.,
October 3, 1960

The communists have nothing but contempt for our courts, our legal profession, our principles of jurisprudence. To them, the Communist Party is the highest law, the tribunal of ultimate appeal. Law is defined and executed by the discipline of the Party. . . .

Law in a communist society is not based on any belief in a Divine Creator, on a body of accepted rules distilled from the experience of men, on norms of fair play, tolerance and free speech. Law as the embodiment of the values of love, justice and truth, as a sinew of understanding among rational men, is unknown. Under communism, law becomes the coercive tool of the communist state. The objective is not impartial justice, the protection of individual liberties or the just settlement of grievances among disputants. . . .

An analysis of communist tactics in undermining the laws of our land should give us an insight into how to cope with this danger. The answer must be an increased reliance on law, a renewed faith in the democratic processes of government.

"Shall It Be Law or Tyranny?" article in *American Bar Association Journal*, February, 1962

In recent years, the communists have demonstrated an attitude of open defiance and contempt for our laws— an attitude which is fortified by their repeated ability to invoke loopholes, technicalities and delays in the law to thwart justice.

Address at Catholic Youth Organization Convention, New York, New York, November 16, 1963

The *political challenge* of communism springs from the Leninist conviction that power, not law, is decisive.

A Study of Communism, page 183

The cumulative effect of almost 50 years of Communist Party activity in the United States cannot be minimized, for it has contributed to disrupting race relations in this country and has exerted an insidious influence on the life and times of our Nation. As a prime example, for years it has been Communist policy to charge "police brutality" in a calculated campaign to discredit law enforcement and to accentuate racial issues. The riots and disorders of the past 3 years clearly highlight the success of this Communist smear campaign in popularizing the cry of "police brutality" to the point where it has been accepted by many individuals having no affiliation with or sympathy for the Communist movement.

1968 FBI Appropriation Testimony, page 59

COMMUNIST EDUCATION

The Communist Party, U.S.A., has created its own educational apparatus for the purpose of indoctrinating Party members and sympathizers, training new cadres of Party leadership, propagandizing noncommunists, and providing centers and rally points for communist activity. Communist schools concentrate on teaching the role that the noncommunist masses can be cleverly induced to play—with the Communist Party as their leader—in obliterating free societies.

The Communist Party conducts training schools for its own members on national, district, state, and local levels. Its students are carefully selected with respect to previous Party experience and training. Schools are held for new members, advanced members, cadres, teachers, trade-union members, Negroes, youth, Party leaders, et cetera. The object, of course, is to make better communist organizers, agitators, and propagandists out of Party members.

* * *

Over the years, the American Communists have developed a propaganda machine and a nefarious and elaborate school system of their own. Their officials in secret and public meetings urge that the propaganda phase of their work must be accelerated. Brazenly, they have urged the development of courses, lectures, and assemblies as media to espouse the ideologies of Marxism and to establish Marxism as a school of thought in the United States.

> Address at Annual Commencement Exercises, Holy Cross College, Worcester, Massachusetts, June 29, 1944

Being good tacticians, the Communists realize that one concealed Party member in education may be worth a dozen in less strategic fields, and some of their more successful propagandists in this area have influenced, and are influencing, the ideas of thousands of impressionable young people.

> "The Communists Are After Our Minds," article in *The American Magazine*, October, 1954

In the Communist Party, education (really meaning indoctrination) is of vital importance. Every member must be deeply imbued with the principles of Marx, Engels, and Lenin.

> Statement by Mr. Hoover concerning the 17th National Convention, Communist Party, U.S.A., December 10–13, 1959, published by the Senate Internal Security Subcommittee

Under communism, education is most definitely not directed toward the interests of the individual. Its primary purpose is none other than to serve as a tool for promoting communist aims. Education is, in such societies, a propaganda weapon designed to help imbue the people with a "high political consciousness," an eagerness and zeal to assist more ably in building the power of communism. There is no room for individuality, only conformity to the demands of the ruthless state.

> "Communism—Slavery of Mind and Spirit," article in *New York State Education*, April, 1962

The Communist world has devised an educational program which is specifically designed to attain world supremacy in science. This educational challenge is one of the most significant aspects of the over-all Com-

munist challenge. The Communist educational program continuously selects the best young minds,
finances their schooling, trains them thoroughly for
specific scientific careers, and offers powerful incentives
to stimulate them to outstanding effort. Under the
current emphasis on scientific training, the student's
life is oriented toward achievement of one goal—attain-
ing scientific and technological progress—and the results are solid evidence that, for Communist purposes,
their educational system is frighteningly effective.

A Study of Communism, page 184

Past ages seem to agree that education should endeavor
to inspire men to superior qualities and point them
toward personal happiness and welfare. In the communist society, however, the good of the state is all;
individual welfare is nothing. Thus, in communist
thinking, education is directed only to training men's
bodies and minds for their role in the state. Since
communism denies the existence of God, there is no
time for men's souls.

"My Answer to Communism and Crime," article in
The Collegiate Challenge, May–June, 1962

Here is a terrifying aspect of Communism—its effort
to indoctrinate the rising generation, to mold these
minds in the atheistic tenets of Marxism-Leninism, to
make them mere soulless cogs of a brutal machine,
where man is degraded and debased.

"The Communist War Against Human Dignity,"
article in *Christian Herald,* July, 1963

Through the dissemination of newspapers, books, pamphlets, leaflets, and other printed matters, the Party indoctrinates its members and sympathizers and is able to reach and propagandize the noncommunist masses. It makes strenuous efforts to increase and expand the distribution and consumption of its literature. . . .

The Party has high hopes of utilizing the interests created by these campus appearances to get a nucleus of students interested in Marxism-Leninism and, subsequently, in a position to be recruited into the Communist Party. While Party leaders understand that they may not have overwhelming success in recruiting the students, they are encouraged over their opportunities to appear on campuses and gain an aura of legitimacy.

1967 FBI Appropriation Testimony, pages 43, 44

AGITATION TACTICS

The object of all communist mass agitation is to develop mass pressure which in turn creates mass action. Mass agitation is usually woven around some definite issue or event, such as the Vietnam war or a racial incident in which "police brutality" is charged. For maximum results, it is an issue which is timely and is being widely discussed.

Communists strive to build mass agitation and pressure around specific issues which will give them the greatest amount of publicity. They inject themselves into issues which will allow them to develop a widening sphere of influence among various segments of the population.

* * *

Every Communist is taught the basic principles of organization, agitation, and propaganda, for the teachings of "Marx, Engels, Lenin, and Stalin . . . enable the Party to direct the struggles of the working class along the correct line and to gain victories while avoiding unnecessary sacrifices." . . .

To that end the Communists are eternally on the alert to mobilize and extend their forces; then either to create or to seize upon a crisis as a springboard to revolution. A Communist pamphleteer proclaimed that they go to legislatures, not to secure legislation to aid capitalism, "but to be a monkey wrench in their machinery, preventing it from working smoothly." A former Communist Party organizer quite openly admitted that a good economic situation does not serve the Communist Party, as it "realizes that a revolutionary movement can only be built among the people who have a grievance, real or imagined or invented."

"Red Fascism in the United States Today," article
in *The American Magazine*, February, 1947

Communism has something to sell to everybody. And, following this principle, it is the function of mass agitation to exploit all the grievances, hopes, aspirations, prejudices, fears, and ideals of all the special groups that make up our society, social, religious, economic, racial, political. Stir them up. Set one against the other. Divide and conquer. That's the way to soften up a democracy.

Masters of Deceit, page 197

To accelerate the revolutionary process, the communists come forth with a plan of action. This includes agitation of the entire social order, the development of class warfare, the use of hatred as a weapon, and the use of people who do not know they are being used to help translate the theory of revolution into the fact of revolution.

"Time of Testing," article in *Christian Action,*
January, 1962

The Communist Party, USA, uses an endless variety of tactics designed to strengthen the Party's influence and to divide, weaken, and confuse anticommunist opposition.

One favorite tactic is the use of "partial" or "immediate" demands. These are short-term demands advanced in order to create favorable conditions for future revolutionary action. They vary greatly in scope and objective and may involve economic, social, political, or cultural issues. . . .

The immediate-demands tactic serves as disguise behind which the Party can carry on ceaseless agitation against our free economy. Even more important, it enables the Party to promote a general feeling of unrest and discontent—to do what the communists term "radicalize" and "politicalize" the masses of people.

> "Deadly Duel," article in *The Airman*, February, 1962

Today, the communists are engaged in a vigorous campaign to divide and weaken America from within. Foremost in this campaign are the Party's efforts to exploit misunderstandings and capitalize upon areas of dissension and unrest wherever they exist. This is especially true in the intense civil rights movement, for America's 20 million Negroes and all others engaged in this struggle are a major target for communist propaganda and subversion.

> Address at Brotherhood of the Washington Hebrew Congregation, Washington, D. C., December 4, 1963

Communists have been deeply interested in student strikes and demonstrations. Not that they have dominated or organized the unrest. Rather, they have sought to utilize it for their own party purposes.

> Interview of Mr. Hoover from *The Napa Register*, Napa, California, May 27, 1965

The Party is working through noncommunist groups and front organizations to embarrass our Government and disrupt its efforts. Communist leaders are striving to initiate other marches and demonstrations to keep their campaign of fear and terror rolling. We can expect that the Party will push for some type of nation-wide action similar to "peace" strikes or work stoppages to emphasize their aims. These are methods which have served communist causes so well since the days of Lenin.

"Message from the Director to All Law Enforcement Officials," *FBI Law Enforcement Bulletin*, June 1, 1965

If by disrupting traffic, heckling prominent individuals, invading Government offices, encouraging civil disobedience, or creating untoward incidents, greater public attention can be attracted—the communists are all for it.

"Reds on Campus," article in *The Daily Texan*, University of Texas, February 21, 1967

Not since the depression of the 1930's has the Communist Party found more fertile fields of agitation. No wonder the party is deeply involved, for example, in the New Left student movement, chiefly through its youth front, the W. E. B. DuBois Clubs. Likewise, though being careful not to be overtly involved, the Party welcomes the tactics of disruption encouraged by civil disobedience and Black Power.

Why? Because it is sincerely interested in improving our society? No. Rather, the party sees New Left-ism, Black Power and civil disobedience as weapons which can be exploited to further a basic aim of Communism, namely the weakening in a democratic society of the citizen's faith in his government, his belief in law and order.

"Violence—A Knife Poised at Heart of U.S.," article in *New York Sunday News*, March 24, 1968

PROPAGANDA

Propaganda has become the most powerful single weapon in the communist arsenal as the means of arousing the masses, luring them toward communism, and preparing and organizing them for revolutionary activity. Propaganda is viewed by communists as a tactic to be used constantly and in close coordination with other tactics. It is utilized both to supplement military, conspiratorial, political, diplomatic, or economic measures, and to substitute for them when these measures are impossible, impractical, unproductive, or uneconomical.

Communist propaganda aimed at the American people is intended to "educate" them along Marxist-Leninist lines and to gain their support in order that they may be maneuvered and mobilized into eventual revolutionary action for the overthrow of the United States Government. No segment of the population and no sphere of activity in this country have been overlooked or neglected by communists as targets for their propaganda.

United States involvement in the war in Vietnam was a signal for communist propagandists to mount a huge campaign to foster the impression that deep-

seated and widespread opposition to the war—especially noncommunist opposition—exists in the United
States. This was to encourage the enemy to prolong the
war in the hope and expectation that mounting adverse
American public opinion would eventually compel an
American military withdrawal and insure a communist
victory.

* * *

There is one element in connection with the whole
communist creed that I think you ought to keep in
mind. Up until the activities of the communists became worldwide, or even national, so far as Russia was
concerned, there had occurred as overt acts in many
countries the actual use of force or violence. But the
war brought in an instrument of warfare never before
used, on so broad a scale, and that was propaganda.

> Testimony by J. Edgar Hoover before Special
> Committee to Investigate Communist Activities in
> the United States, House of Representatives,
> Seventy-first Congress, Second Session, June 10,
> 1930, page 36

Herein lies the greatest threat of the foreign isms.
Wily, cunning masters of perversion that they are, with
no regard for truth, they poison and pollute the very
atmosphere of freedom with venomous attacks upon
everything which we hold dear—our flag, our country,
our churches, our homes, our institutions and our
traditions. It is the object of these schemers to raise
doubt in the minds of our misinformed citizens, who

too frequently follow the leader for the mere purpose of gaining some recognition. The propaganda machine of communism has already demonstrated its tactics. Thoroughly discredited, organization after organization has fallen by the sidelines, once its red tinge became apparent.

Remarks delivered at the Annual Americanization Day Program of The American Legion, Arlington County, Virginia, April 26, 1940

Their aim—the destruction of the power of religion and the establishment of a godless, atheistic society—has not changed. Only their propaganda line has undergone alteration. Now they, the most reactionary advocates of tyranny the world has ever known, best described by the phrase "Red Fascists," advertise themselves as the champions of liberty. They claim to stand for equal rights, for better working conditions, for the abatement of poverty, for the equitable division of the products of industry and for the rights of racial groups and political minorities. But all those idealistic objectives for which all God-fearing people stand are but a cover to conceal their real aims of undermining democracy.

Lecture prepared for delivery at the Conference of Methodist Ministers, Garrett Institute, Evanston, Illinois, November 26, 1947

The inroads that communist propaganda has made in influencing law-abiding Americans, who fail to realize that criminal conspiracies are conceived behind closed doors under the cover of darkness, are disheartening. It is through the efforts of confidential informants that we have been able to expose the communist conspiracy in the past and through them we must stake much of the future security of the United States. That is why such a vicious and sustained attack has been made against former communists who have first-hand knowledge of the secret, diabolical purposes of the Communist Party.

Speech before the International Association of Chiefs of Police Annual Meeting, Philadelphia, Pennsylvania, October 3, 1955

Communist propaganda is tailored to attract noncommunists. Communism offers a bogus "spiritual appeal," a "Kingdom of God on earth." Its tactics and strategy are covered with attractive, appealing words, such as "freedom," "justice," and "equality." The communists claim they are working for a "better world," that they have the answer to discrimination, exploitation, and economic want. To fight for communism, they say, is to become part of the most sacred crusade in the history of man.

Masters of Deceit, page 93

Measured in terms of its subtlety, diversity, vigor, and extent, the world-wide communist propaganda campaign must be rated a substantial one. No medium is overlooked in extolling the merits of communism while at the same time, exploiting social, political, and economic unrest throughout the noncommunist world.

Radio, television, motion pictures, and all forms of the printed word are correlated with such tactics as diplomatic measures, trade agreements, offers of economic and technical assistance, and international trade fairs to subject the Free World to a continuous propaganda barrage. Employed in close conjunction and coordination with communist economic and political machinations, propaganda, one of the most powerful weapons in the communist arsenal, becomes even more formidable. Woven around the themes of peaceful coexistence and peaceful competition, this campaign of psychological pressure can be expected to increase substantially in both variety and intensity in the years to come. . . .

Communist propaganda portrays peace, social progress, and economic prosperity as characteristic of the communist world and claims that these make communist nations invincible. The noncommunist world, on the other hand, is pictured as seething with political instability, economic exploitation, and social upheaval. By identifying the communist world as the hero and the Free World as the villain in the drama of historical progress, communist propaganda represents the triumph of communism, not only as an inevitability, but also as the victory of good over evil.

"Communist Illusion and Democratic Reality," December, 1959 (pamphlet)

The Communists work untiringly to change our form of government while, at the same time, they attempt to be accepted as legitimate partners in our society and to achieve respectability. Not only young people, but all Americans should be cognizant of the party's propagandizing and should be alert to the falsities of the Communist claims. Nothing can defeat this Communist propaganda offensive more quickly than the truth.

1966 FBI Appropriation Testimony, page 65

There are those who say that it is proper and fitting for the Communists to present their views before student groups. We all believe in academic freedom but this does not grant license to deliberately present distortions or falsehoods. Communists are not obligated morally or otherwise to seek for or to tell the truth. Some young people are capable of recognizing and exposing propaganda and propagandists. Others are not. This is the dangerous thing, particularly when it is recognized that the Communists in this country are conducting an energetic propaganda campaign to recruit young people to the Communist banner.

1968 FBI Appropriation Testimony, page 53

INFILTRATION TACTICS

Infiltration is one of the oldest and most widely used of communist tactics, long advocated by communist leaders and theorists. Infiltration gives the Communist Party a foothold among noncommunists, helping communists to disseminate their propaganda and to extend their influence in areas of society which would normally be closed to overt communist activity.

The Party seeks to infiltrate labor unions, the government, civic and community organizations, religious, professional, economic, and social organizations. Its purpose, of course, is to make these organizations serve Party interests wherever possible.

* * *

The Communists know that actual numbers is not the controlling key of the situation, but power is. For that reason the Communists are interested in infiltrating into the most vital industries of the Nation—steel, automobile, coal, rubber. One member in a strategic location is worth ten members elsewhere. He is in a position to wreak, if the situation arose, great industrial damage to our economy. Not only that, but a Communist once in a vital spot can, through his influence, help another Communist gain employment there.

"Foe to Freedom," article in *The Elks Magazine,*
October, 1950

"Let's infiltrate non-Communist groups. Let them do our work." This is today the Communist strategy. They want you, the loyal citizen of the Nation, to promote their unholy cause. Sounds fantastic, doesn't it? But it's true. That is what they are doing today. Communists are trying to join legitimate organizations —a women's community club, a youth organization, a parents' study group. They are working hard, taking an active interest. Why? To gain control of the organization? No. The Communists are few in number, probably one, two or even three. They desire, rather, to influence policy: perhaps elect a "favorable" candidate, determine a policy decision, postpone action on an anti-Communist proposal. In this way, by being "inside" a legitimate organization, they are misguiding many unsuspecting loyal citizens into support of policies fostered by the Communists.

"Make the Communists Show Their Own Colors!" prepared for the International News Service, April 18, 1952

Infiltration is the method whereby Party members move into noncommunist organizations for the purpose of exercising influence for communism.

Masters of Deceit, page 213

Most important is the tactic of infiltration. The placing of communists in organizations—such as civic, religious, and economic groups, as well as labor unions—is an effective technique in spreading "the great ideas of Marxism-Leninism." The dictum of Lenin that communists must "learn to penetrate into prohibited premises where the representatives of the bourgeoisie exercise influence over the workers" is taken most seriously by the Party.

"The Communist Party, USA," article in *Social Order*, September, 1961

The Communist Party works without ceasing to infiltrate labor unions, government, civic and community groups, and to penetrate religious, professional, economic, and social organizations. Its sole purpose in doing so is to achieve some degree of influence in order that the organization can, in various ways, be made to serve Communist Party interests.

"Deadly Duel," article in *The Airman*, February, 1962

The Party is intensifying its campaign to infiltrate and subvert the institutions of our society. The Party's 18th National Convention, for example, specifically spotlighted labor unions as objectives of communist infiltration.

"A Statement on Communism," March 27, 1967 (pamphlet)

LABOR

The Communist Party, U.S.A., in accordance with its claim of being the "political party of the working class," has always regarded labor as its number-one target group. Communists maintain that the "historic mission" of the masses to overthrow the capitalist system cannot be accomplished unless they gain the backing of their most important "ally"—the working class.

Communists recognize that labor unions, with their millions of organized workers, represent dynamic political power which can be harnessed for communist ends. The communist goal in penetrating and capturing trade unions is to convert them into political organizations and then utilize them as instruments for producing the revolutionary overthrow of the United States Government and the seizure of power. Communists seek the cover of labor unions and the support of workers solely to carry out their aim of communizing this country.

* * *

The average American working man is loyal, patriotic and law-abiding. He wants security for his family and himself. But in some unions the rank and file find themselves between a Communist pincers, manipulated by a few leaders who have hoodwinked and browbeaten them into a state of submission.

"Communists Among Us," article in *Washington News Digest,* December, 1946

We, of course, do not investigate labor unions, nor do we concern ourselves with employer-employee relationships. We have, however, investigated innumerable instances of Communist infiltration into labor unions. The Communists today do not have the power that they once had, nor do they have the influence they once had in labor unions. The great majority of labor leaders and organizations are alert to Communist infiltration.

"Communist Threat in U. S.," article in *U. S. News and World Report,* March 30, 1951

Intelligent labor leadership has refrained from fighting Communism with the deceitful tactics employed by the Communists. Instead, this leadership has utilized a weapon unknown to the Communists, yet more deadly than any the Communists have ever devised. That weapon is truth, before which Communism cannot survive—truth about our national institutions, truth about our economic problems, truth about the leadership necessary in labor and management, and, finally, truth about the manifold lies and distortions utilized by the Communists and the system they espouse.

"Red Infiltration of Labor Unions," article in the AF of L *Labor Guide,* Preview Issue, Fall, 1953

Certainly, the Communists' glittering generalities of "freeing the working man" and securing "better working conditions" for him can never take the place of the free bargaining system under our democracy. No semantic window dressing will ever disguise the true objective of communism—to make slaves of working men.

Statement by Mr. Hoover concerning the 17th National Convention, Communist Party, U.S.A., December 10–13, 1959, published by the Senate Internal Security Subcommittee

An overwhelming majority of American labor-union members are honest, hard-working, loyal citizens. They detest communism. This has been proven time after time. Alerted to the presence of communists, they will cast them out. Most of the Party's gains achieved prior to and during World War II in the labor movement have now been destroyed.

Masters of Deceit, page 215

American labor during recent years has done a magnificent job in ousting communists from positions of influence. But, the Party never gives up. It keeps pushing for weak spots, areas where it can influence. We can anticipate that the Party, using the slogan "labor is a key force," will make every effort to recruit industrial workers.

"A Statement on Communism," March 27, 1967 (pamphlet)

FRONT GROUPS

Fronts are an integral part of the communist apparatus throughout the world. To further the cause of communism, noncommunists are relied upon to do the work that communists themselves cannot do as well for many reasons. Communist target groups for fronts are all important segments of society, such as youth, intellectuals, Negroes, foreign born, labor, women, lawyers, teachers. Prominent examples of organizations functioning as fronts in the United States are the W.E.B. DuBois Clubs of America and the American Institute for Marxist Studies.

Through their fronts, communists try to enlist the support of and to manipulate a variety of noncommunists—progressives, liberals, reformists, pacifists, humanitarians, et cetera. Pains are taken to conceal the communist character of the front organizations. Communists give fronts innocuous names and seemingly orthodox and meritorious programs. Every effort is made by communists to place notable and distinguished persons in fronts in order to capitalize on their propaganda value.

*   *   *

The united-front program of the Communist Party was launched at the Seventh World Congress of the Communist International in 1935. The Communist Party in the United States immediately took up the program and a systematic plan was worked out of infiltrating existing organizations with Communists.

For the most part, front organizations assumed the character of either a mass or membership organization or a paper organization. Both solicited and used names of prominent persons. Literally hundreds of groups and organizations have either been infiltrated or organized primarily to accomplish the purposes of promoting the interests of the Soviet Union in the United States, the promotion of Soviet war and peace aims, the exploitation of Negroes in the United States, work among foreign-language groups, and to secure a favorable viewpoint toward the Communists in domestic, political, social, and economic issues.

Statement by J. Edgar Hoover before the House Committee on Un-American Activities, March 26, 1947, relative to the menace of communism

Of all the mass techniques which the Reds are using to influence the minds of Americans, the Communist fronts are the most effective. A Communist front is any organization or movement controlled by the Party. It may be local, state-wide, or national in character; may be large or small; and may exist for years or only for a few days. But in every case the objective of the front organizers is to surround themselves with respectable non-Communists and use them to advance a Party program or spread Red propaganda.

"The Communists Are After Our Minds," article in The American Magazine, October, 1954

A front is an organization which the communists openly or secretly control. The communists realize that they are not welcome in American society. Party influence, therefore, is transmitted, time after time, by a belt of concealed members, sympathizers, and dupes. Fronts become transmission belts between the Party and the noncommunist world.

Masters of Deceit, page 228

Literally hundreds of communist front groups come into being, serve their purpose and then disappear. The danger from such groups rests not so much in their size or in length of life, but in their ability to deceive. Through "fronts" the Party is able to exert influence on thousands of noncommunists, collect immense sums of money, and enlist the minds, pens, and tongues of many distinguished individuals who simply do not know they are dueling in behalf of the communist conspirators.

"Deadly Duel," article in *The Airman,* February, 1962

Over the years the Communist Party, USA, has carried on many of its operations through front organizations established for the purpose, or through the infiltration of legitimate existing organizations.

Through these organizations, the party conducts pressure campaigns, disseminates Communist propaganda, distributes Communist literature, raises funds, and insidiously exploits the masses and public opinion to further its revolutionary aims and purposes.

1963 FBI Appropriation Testimony, page 51

The whole problem of potential ideological violence becomes more serious since the most potent organization, the Communist Party, has mastered the technique of camouflaging its advocacy of force and violence, providing a cover behind which it can develop new strength, both in membership and influence, which may enable it to attain sufficient potency to seize state power. In communism this technique is called "Aesopian language," that is, the use of roundabout or elusive words to conceal the Party's real intentions of violence —words which the "initiated" fully understand in their Marxist-Leninist meanings while the general public is fooled. Hence, the Party is able to operate "fronts," form alliances with noncommunist groups, and encourage citizens to drop their fear of communism. Under the cover of "Aesopian language," the Party is able to draw money, talent and influence for its cause from noncommunist elements of society. The paradoxical situation arises that noncommunists, who actually have no sympathy with communism, are manipulated to support its objectives, enabling the Party to accumulate power for future strikes against our society.

"Violence in American Society—A Problem of Critical Concern," article in *The George Washington Law Review*, Washington, D. C., December, 1967

MINORITY GROUPS

Communists adapt their agitation and propaganda to the fears, prejudices, problems, and special grievances or aspirations of the many ethnic, racial, and religious groups to be found in this country. They endeavor constantly to indoctrinate and mobilize these minority groups so that they can be used to exert pressure on the United States Government to attain desired communist objectives.

Communist agitation and propaganda are especially geared to exploit and accentuate the frictions and differences between the native-born and foreign-born, whites and Negroes, and Jews and Christians solely for the purpose of projecting a political and ideological cohesiveness which will align minority groups with the communist movement.

* * *

The communists have no sincere appreciation of the problems of the Negro, or any sincere desire to help him.

Testimony by J. Edgar Hoover before Special Committee to Investigate Communist Activities in the United States, House of Representatives, June 10, 1930, Seventy-first Congress, Second Session, page 37

The Communist Party from its very inception has held itself out as the "vanguard of the working class," and as such has sought to assume the role of protector and champion of minorities. It directs special attention, among others, to Negroes and nationality groups. Actually the vast majority of Negroes and members of foreign-language groups have rejected communism for what it is: a heartless, totalitarian way of life which completely disregards the dignity of man.

Masters of Deceit, page 243

The Party's claim that it is working for Negro rights is a deception and a fraud. The Party's sole interest, as most American Negroes know, is to hoodwink the Negro, to exploit him and use him as a tool to build a communist America.

Ibid., page 246

Let me emphasize that the American civil rights movement is not, and has *never* been, dominated by the communists . . . *But there are notable exceptions—*dangerous opportunists and morally corrupt charlatans who would form an alliance with any organization, regardless of its nature, to advance their own power and prestige.

Remarks before the Pennsylvania Society and the Society of Pennsylvania Women, New York, New York, December 12, 1964

Historically, the party has exploited minority groups. It hypocritically clamors for an end to discrimination while, at the very same time, it shamelessly practices racial discrimination within its own ranks.

"The Communist Party Line," September 23, 1961, prepared by Mr. Hoover and published by the Senate Internal Security Subcommittee

Special emphasis is placed by the party on penetrating the major Negro protest and improvement associations in an effort to exploit all controversial or potentially controversial racial issues. However, one of the bitterest disappointments of the Communists has been their failure to lure any significant number of our Negro citizens into the party.

A Study of Communism, page 169

The riots and disturbances of recent years have given Communists a golden opportunity to emphasize the Marxist concept of the "class struggle" by identifying the Negro and other minority group problems with it. Communists seek to advance the cause of communism by injecting themselves into racial situations and in exploiting them (1) to intensify the frictions between

Negroes and whites to "prove" that the discrimination
against minorities is an inherent defect of the capitalist
system, (2) to foster domestic disunity by dividing
Negroes and whites into antagonistic, warring factions,
(3) to undermine and destroy established authority,
(4) to incite Negro hostility toward law and order, (5)
to encourage and foment further racial strife and riot-
ous activity, and (6) to portray the Communist movement as the "champion" of social protest and the only
force capable of ameliorating the conditions of the
Negroes and the oppressed.

1968 FBI Appropriation Testimony, page 59

Communists labor ceaselessly to exploit the racial situation and to incite racial strife and violence in this
country. They have been active in exploiting propa-
gandawise the riots of recent years. One main communist goal is to alienate Negroes from established authority.

Statement of J. Edgar Hoover, Director, Federal
Bureau of Investigation, before National Commis-
sion on the Causes and Prevention of Violence,
September 18, 1968

COMMUNISM AND YOUTH

From its earliest days the international
communist movement has exhibited an intense interest
in the youth of all countries. The reason is obvious, for
he who controls the youth controls the future. Com-

munists are forever boasting that communism is "the wave of the future" and "the future belongs to the youth."

No opportunity is overlooked by communists to appeal to and manipulate the credulity, imagination, and fire of youth, particularly college students. Communists are well aware of youth's response to the emotional and idealistic appeal of working toward the betterment of mankind. Communists have been active in organizing and mobilizing young people for civil rights demonstrations, protest activity on college campuses, and demonstrations opposing United States action in Vietnam.

*   *   *

The importance which the Communists place on youth work is reflected by a Party lecture outline in a youth leadership course which concludes with the admonition, "We need a Communist youth movement which can furnish leadership for mass work."

"Red Fascism in the United States Today," article in *The American Magazine*, February, 1947

You, the college student, whether or not you realize it, are the rich earth which the Communist conspirator hopes to till. Your mind is the soil in which he hopes to implant alien seed. Your subsequent acts are the products whose growth he strives to direct. The harvest which he seeks is the destruction of our democratic processes of government.

"Communism and the College Student," article in Boston University *Campus*, March, 1953

If our young citizens turn an objective, analytical searchlight on this ideology and its organizational arms, they will understand communism for what it is—a materialistic, godless dogma dedicated to world domination.

"Message from the Director to All Law Enforcement Officials," *FBI Law Enforcement Bulletin*, October 1, 1964

Most vital is the Party's program among young people, the working with youthful minds to influence them toward communism. "We must develop, train and draw in younger forces. . . ."

The communist program is especially directed toward college groups. Here the Party is today conducting an aggressive campaign for the allegiance of the minds of our young people. They view with optimism their possibilities among students. Young people's interest in the ideas of Marxism-Leninism, the communists insist, is definitely increasing.

"The Communist Party, USA," article in *Social Order*, September, 1961

The intensified drive of the party to attract youth continues unabated. Always anxious to spread its venom on college campuses across the Nation, it has launched an all-out campaign designed to lure youth into the web of communism. This is being done by having more national party functionaries appear before various student groups at various universities.

The party welcomes the opportunity to speak before student groups because it gives the party an aura of respectability; an opportunity to plant seeds of dissent in the minds of individuals; and an opportunity to recruit some youthful followers.

> 1963 FBI Appropriation Testimony, page 50

The widespread communist effort to "hook" American youth is not lessening. On the contrary, it is intensifying. I am confident, however, that the youth of America will faithfully fulfill their responsibilities during this crucial time of testing.

> "Time of Testing," article in *Christian Action*, January, 1962

Why are the communists today appealing so strongly to young people? Why are they encouraging high-level Party officials to speak to student groups? Why are they organizing communist youth organizations? Why do they publish periodicals designed for youth?

The communists realize that the young people will be the leaders of tomorrow. They want to influence their thinking now, to convince them that communism is superior to free government.

> "Statement on Communism," July 15, 1962 (pamphlet)

Intensive efforts are being exerted by the Party to expand its deadly influence among our young people. Communist leaders have devoted much time and work to developing a national youth organization called the W.E.B. DuBois Clubs of America. This organization, which has set up clubs on various college campuses, is purportedly designed to provide a forum for youth interested in socialism. Behind the scenes, the Communist Party, USA, directs its format and looks on it as a device for recruiting new members into the Communist fold.

> "America's Ideals—Its Mark of Greatness," article in *The Union Central Advocate,* 1965 issue

In the Party's opinion, young people today are more receptive to the communist point of view than at any time since World War II. The communists seek to exploit, for their own selfish advantage, what they feel is a restlessness, uncertainty, and aimlessness among many youth in today's complex world. Hence, the future will see renewed Party efforts in this field.

> Interview of Mr. Hoover in *The Christian Science Monitor,* July 3, 1965

Regarding our youth as a formless but pliable mass which can be shaped or molded, the Communist Party, U. S. A., has made clear its purpose and interests. The language jargon utilized is directed toward a single aim —the inculcation in young minds of a perverted theological faith in the ideals and objectives of a Communist society.

> 1966 FBI Appropriation Testimony, page 55

The Communist Party, USA, as well as other subversive groups, is jubilant over these new rebellious activities. The unvarnished truth is that the communist conspiracy is seizing this insurrectionary climate to captivate the thinking of rebellious-minded youth and coax them into the communist movement itself or at least agitate them into serving the communist cause. This is being accomplished primarily by a two-pronged offensive—a much-publicized college speaking program and the campus-oriented communist W. E. B. DuBois Clubs of America. Therefore, the communist influence is cleverly injected into civil disobedience and reprisals against our economic, political, and social system.

"Message from the Director to All Law Enforcement Officials," *FBI Law Enforcement Bulletin,* February 1, 1966

A few students are choosing the communist way, but the vast majority has rejected this alien ideology. The college student is learning to think for himself. He has basic respect for law and order. His life on a college campus is giving him the tools of knowledge and conviction to prevent him from being misled by communists. America should be proud of its rising college generation.

"Reds on Campus," article in *The Daily Texan,* University of Texas, February 21, 1967

COMMUNISM AND THE NEW LEFT

The New Left, which is amorphous and undisciplined, is distinguishable from the communist left, which consists of such authoritarian and dedicated organizations as the pro-Soviet Communist Party, U.S.A., the Red Chinese-oriented Progressive Labor Party, and the Trotskyite Socialist Workers Party. The New Left, however, is not anticommunist and it frequently cooperates with the communist left because of an affinity of goals and interests.

Communists recognize that the New Left represents a reservoir of student power which can be useful to the Party. Accordingly, the Party has increased its participation in New Left activities, particularly anti-Vietnam war demonstrations, and is trying to exploit the New Left to the fullest extent by influencing, manipulating, and directing its activities wherever possible.

The orderly process of education was disrupted at Columbia University in early 1968 and at many other college campuses by student revolts instigated by elements of the New Left. These actions have been fully endorsed and supported by the Party.

* * *

The party has been watching with uninhibited glee the rise of so-called "new left" organizations and groups, which have culminated in "peace" marches, protest demonstrations against American policy in Vietnam, and turmoil on college and university campuses. The party press has carried articles on the "new left," saying the party should guide, exploit, and, if possible, corral this youthful sentiment—which so largely is directed against the "status quo" and the "establishment" and has even encouraged civil disobedience.

> Statement by Mr. Hoover concerning the 18th National Convention, Communist Party, U.S.A., June 22–26, 1966, published by the Senate Internal Security Subcommittee

Here is the danger—that a disciplined, experienced revolutionary organization, like the Communist Party, will be able to reach into the variegated, at times almost chaotic, New Left movement, recruit young people, and then train them into revolutionary cadres. Remembering the words of Lenin, the Party realizes that revolutionary zeal, vociferous and outspoken, is not of great value unless it is channeled into revolutionary cadres—the dedicated men and women who are trained for revolution. The tumultuous unpredictability of some of the New Left leaders makes the Party distrustful of them; but the New Left as a movement has given the Party an ideological bonanza undreamed of just a few years ago.

> "An Analysis of the New Left: A Gospel of Nihilism," article in *Christianity Today,* August 18, 1967

The DuBois Clubs, because it is made up of young communists, has been utilized by the Communist Party to work with the New Left Movement, particularly on the campus, and influence it toward its line of thinking. This organization, hand in hand with the primary spokesman of the New Left, the Students for a Democratic Society, has encouraged youth to resist the draft and subject the Selective Service System to harassment and agitation.

1969 FBI Appropriation Testimony, page 58

The main thrust of the New Left movement arises from the concerted efforts of the Students for a Democratic Society. Many of its members and some of its national leaders openly profess their faith in communist concepts and their determination to "restructure" our society. One of the militant spokesmen of this group stated, for example, that "perhaps twenty-five universities linked to the movement would be too much for the police—for the dominant class—and we would get what we demand."

"Message from the Director to All Law Enforcement Officials," FBI Law Enforcement Bulletin, September 1, 1968

COMMUNIST PARTY LINE

The Communist Party line promises all things to all men. It is skillfully designed to appeal to people from every walk of life, and at the same time to confuse the public by blending proposals ostensibly sponsored by communists with those by noncommunists.

A favorite communist tactic is the policy of "partial" or "immediate" demands. These are the short-term or temporary demands which communists advance in order to create favorable conditions for future revolutionary action. These demands vary greatly in scope and objective. They may be local, regional, national, or international in range. They may be of interest to a large majority of the population or only to a limited minority group. They may vary in significance from a proposal relating to world peace to a demand for low-cost housing. These demands play a vital role in the Communist Party line at any given time.

* * *

The Communist Party line changes from day to day. The one cardinal rule that can always be applied to what the party line is or will be is found in the fundamental principle that the support of Soviet Russia is the duty of Communists of all countries.

One thing is certain. The progress which all good citizens seek, such as old-age security, houses for veterans, and a host of others, is being adopted as window dressing by the Communists to conceal their true aims and entrap gullible followers.

"Communism in the United States," article in *Confidential—from Washington,* June, 1948

The forces which are most anxious to weaken our internal security are not always easy to identify. Communists have been trained in deceit and secretly work toward the day when they hope to replace our American way of life with a Communist dictatorship. They utilize cleverly camouflaged movements, such as some peace groups and civil rights organizations, to achieve their sinister purposes. While they as individuals are difficult to identify, the Communist Party line is clear. Its first concern is the advancement of Soviet Russia and the godless Communist cause. It is important to learn to know the enemies of the American way of life.

"Statement of J. Edgar Hoover, Director, Federal
Bureau of Investigation," July 26, 1950 (pamphlet)

On both the local and national levels, the Communist Party, USA, is continually exploiting social, economic, and political grievances for its own tactical purposes. For this reason, the "Party line" will frequently coincide with the views of many noncommunists on specific issues. We must not, therefore, indiscriminately label as communists those whose opinions on a particular question may, on occasion, parallel the official Party position. We must also guard against the tendency to characterize as communists those who merely disagree with us or who advocate unorthodox or unpopular beliefs.

"Communist Illusion and Democratic Reality," December, 1959 (pamphlet)

The term "party line" is frequently used by Americans in talking about communism. Too often the term is used loosely to denote "following a certain line of action" or set of party demands.

In communism, however, the party line plays a highly significant and specific role—a vital part in the party's program for the revolutionary overthrow of our form of government. We, as Americans, should know more about the party line. What is it? How is it formed? How does it operate? As citizens we should know how to understand and interpret the party line—realizing that it is a hypocritical and deceitful technique to hoodwink and beguile us. The great danger today is that the constant reiteration of the party line by Communists— day after day—may cause their demands to be accepted as valid and truthful.

The party line, in fact, is the sum total of all party demands at any given time. These demands, whether they are local, national, or international in nature, are designed to promote the Communist revolution. However vehemently the Communists may campaign for the various proposals which compose the party line, they are not genuinely interested in "reforms" or improving our society. For the party, reforms are useful only to the extent to which they advance the ultimate revolution. The party regards reforms as temporary, transitional adjustments which can be achieved during a period when the party has not yet attained sufficient strength to risk direct revolutionary action.

> "The Communist Party Line," September 23, 1961, prepared by Mr. Hoover and published by the Senate Internal Security Subcommittee

This barrage of propaganda representing Communist demands is the Communist Party line. The pages of

Communist publications are filled with these demands and the public speeches and statements of party leaders are largely based on them.

However vehemently the Communists may campaign for the various proposals which constitute the party line, they are not genuinely interested in "reforms" or improving our society. Communists declare themselves for a lasting international peace—as long as no one stands up to Communist aggression; for peaceful coexistence—strictly on Communist terms; and for freedom of all people—to live under a Communist dictatorship.

1963 FBI Appropriation Testimony, page 51

The policies of the Party in this country are, as always, a determined effort to follow a Party line as dictated by its Soviet masters. The rigidity with which the Communist Party—USA follows the Moscow line was well demonstrated in the position taken by the Party after the Middle East crisis in the Summer of 1967. Despite the hue and cry of many of its members with Jewish backgrounds, the Communist Party—USA faithfully followed the Moscow line in branding Israel as the aggressor and the tool of "American imperialism."

1969 FBI Appropriation Testimony, page 48

ESPIONAGE

The USSR has organized the largest and most formidable espionage and intelligence system in history and maintains an unprecedented network of spies around the world. Since the United States is the main adversary of communism, we are naturally the primary target of communist-bloc spying.

During the 1920's, 1930's, and early 1940's the American communist movement furnished considerable spy talent. But gradually, over a period of years, the role of the Communist Party, U.S.A., underwent a change. Foreign communist agents depended less and less on the Party's direct ability to facilitate espionage operations. The "drawing away" from the Party by these foreign agents was strictly a tactical maneuver, however. High selectivity in the use of Communist Party members for espionage work afforded greater security not only to their own operations but also to the Party's subversive activities.

* * *

There are, of course, other individuals, who are not directly connected with the Communist Party, but who are sympathetic to their aims, or who are sympathetic to the operation of the Soviet Government who, therefore, assist in espionage activities and in subversive propaganda initiated by foreign governments.

1951 FBI Appropriation Testimony, page 739

Thus, the fact remains that the basic principles of Marxist-Leninist philosophy, demanding the use of force and violence, represent the guides for commu-

nism to achieve world conquest. The extensive espionage activities directed against the United States
which, in the past, have utilized communists and communist sympathizers in this country as well as other
individuals who could be subverted, can be better
understood when regarded as essential tools in the relentless and fanatical drive of international communism
to conquer the world.

"Exposé of Soviet Espionage," May, 1960, prepared
by Mr. Hoover and published by the Senate Internal Security Subcommittee

American workmen who are producing the materials
and weapons for our defense can be our best guardians
against sabotage and espionage. Among the prime targets of foreign-directed espionage are our major defense
industries, and alert workmen at these installations can
greatly assist in the protection of our defense secrets
by promptly reporting any indication of sabotage or
espionage.

"Statement on Internal Security," April 17, 1961
(pamphlet)

Numerous intelligence-gathering sources make up the
highly integrated Soviet-bloc espionage apparatus.
Covert intelligence collection is accomplished under
the cover of every Russian-run establishment in the
United States. Other operatives function clandestinely
under false identities without any observable contact
with the official establishments. As a part of the overall
apparatus, the Soviets greatly increase their intelligence

collection potential by pressing into their service the foreign intelligence facilities of their satellite nations in the United States as well as in other parts of the world. The Soviets not only have access to all data obtained by the satellites but they also maintain an advisor system at satellite headquarters level to make certain that the satellites operate consistent with Soviet interests.

1963 FBI Appropriation Testimony, pages 52–53

Targets of Soviet-bloc intelligence and espionage activities in the United States are all-embracing. Many targets are predictable, such as defense plans, or information about weapons development, deployment of military personnel, strategic military and industrial areas, and scientific and industrial advances. Efforts are also made to penetrate government agencies, to ascertain United States foreign policy, and to gather information about anti-Communist emigre groups in the United States.

A Study of Communism, page 174

Regardless of the secrecy and care with which Soviet-bloc intelligence and espionage operations proceed, their role is to sap the strength of this nation while vitalizing the Communist machine in its efforts to control the world. Like all Communist operations, they are designed to carry out the mandate of the 1960 statement of the 81 Communist parties—to disrupt and weaken the influence and strength of the United States.

Ibid., page 181

The fact is that the Party in this country functions as a valuable auxiliary of the Soviet-bloc espionage network! From their areas of influence, American communists have produced a Julius Rosenberg, a Morton Sobell, and others both willing and able to betray vital secrets to the Soviet Union.

> Address at The American Legion Convention, Las Vegas, Nevada, October 9, 1962

The United States is today Soviet Spy Target No. 1. Never in history has a nation been under such highly organized and competent spy attack.

> "The U.S. Businessman Faces the Soviet Spy," article in *Harvard Business Review*, January–February, 1964

A growing problem is the extent to which the Soviet intelligence services are dispatching undercover spies into the United States. These individuals have no ostensible connection with either the official Soviet establishments or personnel in this country nor do they make any overt contacts with their foreign espionage headquarters. They are well-trained, professional intelligence officers and usually bear assumed identities and are supplied with expertly fabricated documents and unlimited funds. They enter the United States without difficulty to become assimilated into our population and, unless uncovered, eventually serve as the nucleus of an extensive clandestine espionage network.

> 1966 FBI Appropriation Testimony, page 69

Soviet espionage in this country is today being committed by highly professional, well-trained agents who
. . . are suave, articulate, aggressive, poised, who speak
English well and are conversant with American cus-
toms, thereby enabling them to make effective direct
and personal contacts with American businessmen, industrial executives and employees.

> "The Modern-Day Soviet Spy—A Profile," article in
> *Industrial Security,* August, 1966

The tempo of the multipronged espionage attack
against this Nation continues to increase. This concerted drive is evidenced not only in increased activity
from the Soviets, their satellites and other communist-
bloc countries, but also in significantly stepped-up
drives from Castro's Cuba and from Red China.

We must provide wide coverage of all these sources
of espionage since all possible avenues available to them
are being utilized in their efforts to penetrate the national defense interests of the United States. Spies on
intelligence missions for their governments enter this
country under every conceivable cover. They are found
among the official diplomatic representatives of their
countries. They enter as students, tourists, commercial
representatives and members of cultural exchange
groups. They infiltrate with refugees and emigres.

> 1969 FBI Appropriation Testimony, page 67

Combating Communism

COMMUNISM VERSUS
FREEDOM–A CONTRAST

Communism is a direct attack on individual freedom—the very cornerstone of our society. It is a conflict between two diametrically opposed concepts of the meaning of human life itself.

Communism, which is an atheistic and materialistic ideology, claims, in effect, that man is only what he eats; that there is no essential difference—only a difference of degree—between human and other forms of life; that morality is based upon expediency; that history is a purely materialistic process in which the economic factor is decisive; and that the individual exists only for, and is subordinate to, an all-powerful state.

Our way of life, on the other hand, is founded on the conviction that man lives not by bread alone, but also by spiritual values. We hold that every human being has a certain inherent dignity and worth. Because our actions are directed and guided by traditional Judaeo-Christian moral law, we have standards of what is right and what is wrong. Therefore, under freedom, each individual has certain inalienable rights which can never be abrogated by the state.

*   *   *

Both communism and fascism are the antitheses of American belief in liberty and democracy.

> Address before The American Legion Convention, Los Angeles, California, September 19, 1938

The communists would have us believe that freedom can be attained only under their system. Yet, the history of every nation under a communist regime demonstrates conclusively that the communist version of freedom is only a new form of total slavery.

> "One Nation's Response to Communism," September, 1960 (pamphlet)

Throughout history, man has been confronted with a never-ending struggle against tyranny. However, history has shown that free societies have invariably proved more resilient, creative, and enduring than those under a totalitarian yoke. The ultimate guarantee against Communist encroachment is a deep and abiding awareness on the part of each citizen that freedom is inherently superior to communism. Communists falsely pose the issue as one between communism and capitalism. In reality, the struggle is one between freedom and tyranny. And, when communism is finally defeated, it will not be a victory of capitalism over communism or of the United States and its allies over the Communist bloc. It will be the victory of freedom over tyranny.

A Study of Communism, page 190

The Communist party rules through a totalitarian government with absolute powers.	Freedom provides a constitutional government with power derived from the people.
Communism maintains a dictatorship with no regard for the people.	Freedom makes possible a government of, by, and for the people.
The will of the Communist state is supreme.	Under freedom, the will of the people is supreme.

Ibid., page 198

There is a vast difference between Americanism and communism. One teaches morality; the other, expediency. One follows the Law of God; the other, no law. One is founded upon spiritual values; the other is complete secularism. One is characterized by deep religious conviction; the other, by ruthless, atheistic materialism. The communist world is a world of walls, searchlights, and guards—a prison for the heart, mind and soul.

Address at The American Legion Convention, Las Vegas, Nevada, October 9, 1962

If you listen to a communist, he'll exclaim that our system of government cannot meet the test of time. It is, he says, "obsolete," "decadent," "soon to die." He then points with pride to "Marxism," the "system of scientific socialism," which he says will answer all the problems of the future.

Yes, America does have many problems—serious problems. But the answer is not, as the communists assert, a destruction of what we hold dear, our liberties, our freedoms, our concepts of law, but a cooperative spirit of understanding, tolerance and fair play. A free government can surmount these problems—and surmount them in a democratic manner. We must recognize the communist effort for what it is—an effort to inject poison into the bloodstream of America, to confuse, obscure and distort America's vision of itself.

"A Statement on Communism," March 27, 1967 (pamphlet)

THE CITIZEN'S RESPONSIBILITY

We live in a tension-packed atmosphere characterized by alternate periods of storm and calm, but constantly under the cloud of nuclear annihilation. We must continue to be alert and to be prepared for continuing difficulties and confrontations with communism. We must comprehend the totality and the significance of the conflict between communism and freedom, and realize that the outcome will decide what principles and values will determine—perhaps for centuries—the future course of mankind.

To emerge the victor in the fierce struggle now

raging, each citizen must live in accordance with the Judaeo-Christian tradition, show sincere regard for the rights of others, respect the law, champion social justice, and be unswervingly dedicated to the moral and religious principles of Western civilization on which this country was founded.

*   *   *

A good citizen must be on guard against subversion in all its forms. Call it communism, fascism, or what you will—it is un-American. Our patriotism can best be judged by our diligence in protecting American ideals from the rapists of justice and common decency. To stem the insidious machinations of such enemies, to thwart their plans, to preserve our traditions and ideals, is a sacred and supreme task. Here is a battle between priceless God-fearing principles on the one hand and pagan ideals and godlessness on the other. Principles and not men must prevail. Democracy is totally alien in deed and thought to the tactics of ruthless racketeering dictators. Yet that is what these festering foreign isms stand for, while they insult our intelligence and blaspheme Americanism by calling communism "Twentieth Century Democracy." What a travesty!

Remarks at Annual New York Herald-Tribune Forum, New York, New York, October 24, 1939

Western democracy must utilize its vast reservoirs of moral and spiritual strength—the sparks which set the souls of men afire and light the dark path ahead. We can do the job and do it in the American way. There is no need, whatsoever, for an abridgement of civil liberties or the creation of a national police system. The answer to the Communist menace is a thoroughly alert and aroused citizenry, cognizant of the evils of Marxism-Leninism, and ready at all times to work for the promotion of democratic principles. America's belief in free government, in the ability of men through their own conscious efforts to shape their future destinies, is the world's hope of tomorrow. Democracy is the gigantic fulcrum upon which the hopes and aspirations of all men rest. We in America have a tremendous responsibility to ourselves and to countless millions unseen. We must continue to hold the line and wave the banner of freedom on high.

> "Foe to Freedom," article in *The Elks Magazine,* October, 1950

In this age of uncertainty—in this age when the struggle between freedom and totalitarian enslavement is drawing toward a climax—we have need of faith as never before. We have need of faith of the kind which put iron in the souls of our forefathers, enabling them to meet and overcome adversity. We have need of that same faith to fortify ourselves as we meet the communist enemy in today's deadly contest.

> "The Deadly Contest," article in *Columbia* magazine, August, 1961

We must never underestimate the communist menace, yet in the course of combating this deadly enemy ut-

most care is imperative. We can harm ourselves and
our Nation by yielding to the panicky fear which results in hysteria, witch hunts and vigilante activities.
We can do grave injustice to the innocent by repeating
idle rumor and malicious gossip. Indiscriminate inquiries and private investigations similarly can be
harmful to the innocent. In addition, such actions very
well may jeopardize the vital work of responsible security agencies. The person who secures information relative to espionage, sabotage or subversive activities
should report it immediately to the FBI without attempting to take individual action.

> "Communism and The Knowledge To Combat It!"
> article in *The Retired Officer Magazine*, January–
> February, 1962

In fulfilling his responsibility, the individual citizen
must be more than alert to the dangers of communism
and its conspiratorial operations. He must be vitally
concerned with the establishment of measures, on all
levels of American life, which will remedy or improve
those social, psychological, political, and economic
factors exploited by Communists to gain support for
their cause. In this positive manner, Communist efforts
to capitalize on the misfortunes of others will be
thwarted.

> *A Study of Communism*, page 188

Much has been done by the Government's internal
security programs; by investigation, arrest and prosecu-

tion of Party functionaries; and by widespread intelligent public opposition to the Marxist philosophy to thwart the Communist Party's efforts in this country.

However, communism remains an intense subversive threat. Our Nation's efforts to deal effectively with this menace are not enhanced by those of the extreme right who tend to affix the communist label without intelligent analysis, or by those of the extreme left who endeavor to minimize the real danger of communism.

Address at The American Legion Convention, Las Vegas, Nevada, October 9, 1962

Our approach toward communism must not be negative or defeatist. We are against communism, but that is not enough. We must stand for something—the moral and spiritual forces which make for decency, honesty, and understanding. These ideals are what give strength to America.

"The U. S. Businessman Faces the Soviet Spy," article in *Harvard Business Review*, January–February, 1964

Alert yourself—learn the true nature and tactics of communism.

Make civic programs for social improvement your business.

Exercise your right to vote; elect representatives of integrity.

Respect human dignity—communism and individual rights cannot coexist.

Inform yourself; know your country—its history, traditions, and heritage.

Combat public apathy toward communism—indifference can be fatal when national survival is at stake.

Attack bigotry and prejudice wherever they appear; justice for all is the bulwark of democracy.

> "What You Can Do to Fight Communism" (poster, April, 1959)

This attitude can be seen in the widespread public indifference concerning the real threat of world communism. The philosophy of communism flourishes best in an environment where personal responsibility and self-discipline have been undermined by immorality, materialism and expediency.

> Remarks upon receiving Sword of Loyola Award, Chicago, Illinois, November 24, 1964

America must roll up its sleeves and face the communist danger. Theodore Roosevelt, that great American, stated: "Much has been given us, and much will rightfully be expected from us. We have duties to others and duties to ourselves; and we can shirk neither."

Here is the challenge—we cannot shrink from the duties and responsibilities which are ours in mid-twentieth century America. We have a great heritage of freedom to protect. The times call for courage, resolution and integrity, not cleverness, expediency or love of soft living. No man has a right to a "time out," "a leave of absence"—all must be on the front lines.

> "A Statement on Communism," March 27, 1967 (pamphlet)

ABOUT THE AUTHOR

JOHN EDGAR HOOVER was born in the District of Columbia on January 1, 1895. He was educated in the District of Columbia and earned the Bachelor of Laws and Master of Laws degrees at The George Washington University. He entered the Department of Justice in 1917. Two years later he was named Special Assistant to the Attorney General, in which capacity he began his penetrative study of the newly formed Communist Party. In 1921 Mr. Hoover was appointed Assistant Director of the Bureau of Investigation—the name by which the FBI then was known. He became Director on May 10, 1924, and has served in that position continuously since. Under Mr. Hoover's expert administration, the FBI has pioneered many of the most important developments in twentieth-century crime detection and has achieved a position of international respect and acclaim in both the investigative and counterintelligence fields. A recognized authority on the problems of crime and subversion, Mr. Hoover has written three previous books: *Persons in Hiding*, 1938; *Masters of Deceit*, 1958; and *A Study of Communism*, 1962.